Locke

"Edward Feser provides an excellent introduction to the philosophy of John Locke, who 'made a bigger difference to the whole intellectual climate of mankind than anyone since Aristotle' (Gilbert Ryle). Especially illuminating is Feser's account of the relation between Locke's liberal political philosophy and his empiricist epistemology and metaphysics."

Fred Miller – Social Philosophy and Policy Center,
Bowling Green State University

"The book opens the door on Locke's thinking as if on a long dormant factory whose machinery is still gleaming and ready to run ... striking and instructive."

Graeme Hunter – Professor of Philosophy, Ottawa University, Canada

THE *ONEWORLD THINKERS* SERIES:

Each book in the *Oneworld Thinkers* series introduces the life and works of a major intellectual figure, exploring their most influential ideas and their lasting legacy. Accessibly written by prominent academics, the books in this series are a must-have for anyone interested in ideas.

Currently Available

Dennett
Tadeusz Zawidzki
ISBN 978–1–85168–484–7

Hume
Harold Noonan
ISBN 978–1–85168–493–9

Locke
Edward Feser
ISBN 978–1–85168–489–2

Nietzsche
Robert Wicks
ISBN 978–1–85168–485–4

Rawls
Paul Graham
ISBN 978–1–85168–483–0

Wittgenstein
Avrum Stroll
ISBN 978–1–85168–486–1

Forthcoming

Aquinas
Edward Feser

Berkeley
Harry M. Bracken

Derrida
David Cunningham

Dewey
David Hildebrand

Dostoevsky
Diane Oenning Thompson

Eco
Florian Mussgnug

Habermas
David Ingram

Hobbes
Alistair Edwards

Huxley
Kieron O'Hara

Irigaray
Rachel Jones

Jung
Susan Rowland

Locke

Edward Feser

ONEWORLD THINKERS

ONEWORLD
OXFORD

LOCKE

A Oneworld Book

Published by Oneworld Publications 2007

ISBN-13:978–1–85168–489–2

Typeset by Jayvee, Trivandrum, India
Cover design by Simon McFadden
Printed and bound by TJ International Ltd, Padstow, Cornwall

Oneworld Publications
185 Banbury Road
Oxford OX2 7AR
England
www.oneworld-publications.com

Learn more about Oneworld. Join our mailing list to
find out about our latest titles and special offers at:

www.oneworld-publications.com

Contents

Preface and acknowledgements

Books about Great Dead Philosophers always run the risk of turning them into museum pieces, purveyors of arcane and irrelevant doctrines whose study in the present day can only ever be of antiquarian interest. This danger is especially great in a volume which emphasizes the historical background against which a philosopher wrote and thought. One trend in recent analytic philosophy seeks to avoid this problem by emphasizing instead the ways in which the ideas and arguments of past philosophers might be interpreted so as to be applicable to the problems that interest philosophers today. Here another and opposite danger arises, and analytic historians of philosophy are often accused of distorting the ideas of past philosophers by ignoring the context in which they developed and imposing on them artificial and anachronistic readings.

It is possible, though, to avoid both these extremes, and someone writing on Locke is bound to have an easier time of it than someone writing on a Plotinus or a Schopenhauer. For Locke, as I aim to show, is as clearly relevant to our time as he was to the time in which he wrote. Moreover, this becomes most obvious precisely when we read him in light of the historical background of the ideas against which he was reacting. Locke is one of the key architects, maybe *the* architect, of distinctively modern ways of thinking in philosophy, science, politics, and religion. His ideas, more than those of perhaps any other early modern philosopher, survive in the "mainstream" of Western thought today. Where modern people believe they have moved beyond what they regard as the superstitions of the medieval worldview, they tend to believe this for broadly Lockean reasons. To a very great extent, when they seek to progress even further beyond moral and religious ideas identified as medieval, they again justify their position on broadly Lockean grounds. And when others seek instead to hold back such a development in the interests of maintaining continuity with more ancient and religious ways of thinking, they too typically do so for Lockean reasons. If, as these claims suggest, there are tensions in Locke's philosophy, they are some of the same tensions that characterize contemporary intellectual and political life. Liberals and conservatives, religious believers and skeptics, can all find in Locke much to like and much to dislike; and if the debates between them often seem intractable, that may be precisely because they all have an equally strong claim to the Lockean legacy. To understand Locke is to understand ourselves.

These are large claims, and I hope the chapters that follow will justify them. The reader will find in those chapters a fair amount of discussion of the ideas of the Scholastic and rationalist philosophers who preceded Locke, and also of thinkers who have come after him down to the present day, for you cannot properly understand Locke's ideas or their significance for us today apart from this context. Still, this is a book about Locke, and the reader will, above all, find a solid introduction to Locke's thinking in general philosophy, in politics, and in religion, and be made aware also of the interconnections between his ideas in these different areas. The focus will be on the arguments presented in Locke's three most influential works, the *Essay Concerning Human Understanding*, the *Second Treatise of Government*, and the *Letter Concerning Toleration*, though we will now and again have reason to refer to some of his other works too.

I want to thank Victoria Roddam, the editor with whom I worked out the details of this project, for her interest and encouragement. I also thank my current editor, Martha Jay, and the staff of Oneworld Publications in general, who have, as always, been unfailingly helpful. An anonymous reviewer made several suggestions for improving the manuscript, for which I am grateful. It goes without saying that my beloved wife Rachel and our beautiful children Benedict, Gemma, and Kilian deserve thanks for putting up with Dad when he has for too many hours been hidden away in his office. My parents Edward and Linda Feser were somewhat less aware of my daily labors on this book, but they deserve thanks for making me – and thus it – possible, in so very many ways. It is to them, with love, gratitude, and affection, that I dedicate the book.

System of citations

I have cited editions of Locke's works which are as accessible as possible to students and non-specialists – accessible in the sense of being relatively easy to find in a library or bookstore, and accessible in the sense of being free of archaic spelling, distracting capitalizations of key terms, and the like. This has necessitated departing somewhat from the usual practice of citing the standard scholarly editions, such as P. H. Nidditch's edition of the *Essay* (Oxford: Oxford University Press, 1975) and Peter Laslett's edition of the *Two Treatises* (Cambridge: Cambridge University Press, 1960), but since in most cases the citations are by section numbers rather than page numbers, readers using those editions will have little difficulty in locating the texts cited. The following abbreviations will be used:

E   *An Essay Concerning Human Understanding,* ed. Roger Woolhouse (London: Penguin Books, 1997). References are by book, chapter, and section. "The Epistle Dedicatory" and "The Epistle to the Reader" are referred to by page numbers.

T   *Two Treatises of Government.* In *Two Treatises of Government and A Letter Concerning Toleration*, ed. Ian Shapiro (New Haven and London: Yale University Press, 2003). References are by treatise and paragraph.

ELN   *Essays on the Law of Nature.* In *Locke: Political Essays*, ed. Mark Goldie (Cambridge: Cambridge University Press, 1997). References are by page number.

LT   *A Letter Concerning Toleration.* In *Two Treatises of Government and A Letter Concerning Toleration*, ed. Ian Shapiro (New Haven and London: Yale University Press, 2003). References are by page number.

EPL   *An Essay on the Poor Law.* In *Locke: Political Essays*, ed. Mark Goldie (Cambridge: Cambridge University Press, 1997). References are by page number.

RC   *The Reasonableness of Christianity.* In *John Locke: Writings on Religion*, ed. Victor Nuovo (Oxford: Clarendon Press, 2002). References are by page number.

The Quintessential Modern Philosopher

Locke's significance

Of all modern philosophers, John Locke has had the profoundest influence on the world we live in, and most embodies its guiding principles. Other modern philosophers might have been *greater* philosophers, by whatever standards we are to judge philosophical greatness. Perhaps a Descartes, Hume, or Kant excelled Locke in originality, in depth and breadth of philosophical vision, or even in just getting things right. One could certainly make that case. But no other thinker has been more representative of paradigmatically modern attitudes toward science, politics, and religion, or more directly responsible for shaping those attitudes. Descartes is usually called the father of modern philosophy, and with good reason, but Locke, more than any other philosopher, has a claim to being the father of modernity in general. If we want to understand ourselves, we need to understand him, for our world is to a very great extent a Lockean world.

Modern Westerners do not put much stock in authority or tradition as a source of moral or theoretical guidance, tending instead to regard empirical science as the paradigm of knowledge and rationality. Yet they are, at

1

the same time, inclined to be doubtful that very much in the way of strict knowledge (if that entails certainty) is really possible, even in science. All of these attitudes have their roots in Locke, and find their classic philosophical expression in his *Essay Concerning Human Understanding.* Modern Westerners also tend to combine a very high regard for the freedom of all human beings to practice whatever religion they see fit with a deep skepticism about the objective defensibility of most particular religious dogmas. These too are very Lockean attitudes, and Locke's *Letter Concerning Toleration* did more to propagate them than perhaps any other book.

In no other country are these attitudes more prevalent than in that most Lockean of nations, the United States of America. There too the rhetoric of liberty, whether political, economic, or religious, rings loudest, as does (in some quarters anyway) the theme that a free society rests on the recognition of a divine Lawgiver to whom all people and governments are ultimately answerable. Here perhaps is where Locke's influence on the modern world has been most profound. For the defense of the rights of the individual against the power of the state was the great theme of Locke's *Second Treatise of Government*; and whatever his ambivalence about the theological details on which various religious traditions disagree, he was adamant about the general proposition that those rights have a theological foundation – albeit in a distinctly modern, Enlightenment-style theology with which his medieval predecessors would not have been entirely comfortable. For Locke, whether or not reason can settle disputes between various sects over fine points of doctrine, it can at least reveal to us that there is a God, that that God has granted us certain rights, and that these rights put severe constraints on the ambitions and power of human governments. Prominent among these rights in Locke's account are the rights to private property and, more generally, to the fruits of one's labor, so that the Lockean understanding of rights has always been associated as much with the defense of the modern free market economy as it has with limited government and religious liberty. Through the English political tradition and the impact it has had on the former colonies of the British Empire, and especially through the American founding fathers and the nation they created, all of these ideas were to have a profound impact on the history of the last three centuries.

That this impact is as great today as it ever was is evident from the history of the post-9/11 world. In defending recent American foreign policy, and in particular his administration's commitment to spreading political, religious, and economic freedom around the globe, U. S. president George W. Bush has said repeatedly that "freedom is the almighty God's gift to each man and woman in this world." Some commentators have been prone to dismiss such sentiments as either an unsophisticated throwback to less Enlightened pre-modern times or mere political boilerplate. This is a mistake, and not a small one. In fact, the president's words reflect (whether knowingly or not) the Lockeanism that has frequently underlain American thinking about political matters, and for that very reason they reflect the most influential and sophisticated political theory of the Enlightenment era. Many today, including many intellectuals of a religious bent, still sympathize with this Lockean view of the relationship between politics and theology. Of course, many others find it troubling; certainly the president's rhetoric has been controversial. But whatever one's opinion of these ideas, it is crucial that one properly understand them, and thus that one understand Locke's rationale for approaching questions of political philosophy in the manner he did.

I have said that that rationale is a sophisticated one, but that does not mean that it is unproblematic. Probably the majority of contemporary philosophers would no longer endorse its theological basis, though there are still some who would. Even aside from the question of religious foundations, though, there are significant tensions in the Lockean political project, and they are, by no means coincidentally, some of the very same ones that beset us in contemporary political life: tensions between a modern scientific vision of mankind and a recognition of human dignity and human rights; between a minimalist and empirically-oriented theory of knowledge and ambitious and controversial moral and metaphysical claims about the nature of persons; and between individual liberty of thought and action and the prerequisites of a stable, free, and just society. Whether these tensions can be resolved is not just a question of interest to scholars of Locke's philosophy; it is of great consequence to all of us.

There are well-known problems too with the more technical aspects of Locke's philosophy, namely the epistemological and metaphysical theses with which he sought to provide a philosophical foundation for modern science. Those who value modern science or, more generally, sympathize with the general spirit of Locke's theory of knowledge – empiricist, individualist, anti-authoritarian – need to consider whether something like his way of grounding these things can ultimately be defended. In the intellectual realm as much as in the political realm, Locke's theme was freedom, but a freedom exercised within definite moral and rational constraints. It is important to determine whether Locke's conception of freedom, in either the intellectual or the political sense, ultimately coheres with the constraints he wanted to put on it – and if not, then which element, the freedom or the constraints, ought to be abandoned.

As we will see in the chapters to follow, many of the difficult questions raised by Locke's project derive from his peculiar position in the history of thought. Locke straddles the medieval and post-modern worlds, the age of faith and the age of skepticism and secularism. Locke and his fellow early modern philosophers rejected many elements of the medieval worldview, but maintained others, even if sometimes in an altered form. What we have inherited from these philosophers includes both their rejection of some of these elements and their retention of others, though contemporary thinkers are inclined to reject even more aspects of the medieval inheritance than the early modern ones did. Some crucial questions we will need to consider are whether Locke can consistently reject those aspects of the medieval worldview that he does reject while maintaining the positive claims he wants to defend – and also whether we contemporary Westerners can consistently keep those aspects of our Lockean and medieval inheritances that we like while rejecting those we would rather do without.

Properly to understand Locke's philosophy will in any event require understanding the medieval Scholastic tradition he was reacting against, as well as the philosophical and scientific context of the early modern period that formed the milieu in which he thought and wrote. The next chapter will sketch out this intellectual background, and succeeding chapters will explore the development of Locke's thought in his three most important works, namely the *Essay*, the *Second Treatise*, and the *Letter Concerning Toleration* already mentioned. The final chapter will assess Locke's ultimate significance and continuing relevance for the contemporary world.

Locke's life and character

First, though, a brief look at Locke's life is in order, for the events of that life are by no means irrelevant to an understanding of his work. He was born to Puritan parents of modest means, near Bristol in England, in 1632, the year Galileo published his *Dialogue Concerning the Two Chief World Systems*. In 1652 he began study at Christ Church, Oxford, where he quickly grew dissatisfied with the still-reigning medieval Aristotelianism he was taught; he would later become acquainted with the works of contemporary thinkers like Rene Descartes (1596–1650) and Pierre Gassendi (1592–1655). After graduating, he pursued what was to become a lifelong interest in modern medicine, and also began a friendship with the chemist Robert Boyle (1627–91), one of the great scientists of the age. The Puritan influence, and especially the influence of modern philosophy and modern science, would dramatically shape the philosophical positions Locke was to develop through the course of his life.

In 1666, Locke met Anthony Ashley Cooper, who was later to become the first Earl of Shaftesbury, and began what would be perhaps the most important association of his career. Locke would join Shaftesbury's household in London as his advisor and personal physician, and directed a medical operation which saved Shaftesbury's life. Their friendship was to bring Locke into the center of the political controversies of the day, especially after Shaftesbury began actively opposing the policies of Charles II. The trouble this caused Shaftesbury may have contributed to Locke's decision in 1675 to leave England for France, where for three and a half years he consorted with some of the leading intellectuals of the day.

Not long after Locke's return to England, Shaftesbury was again embroiled in controversy related to his opposition to Charles, who had dissolved Parliament after it attempted to pass a law blocking Charles' Catholic brother James from succeeding him on the throne and reestablishing Catholic control over England. Shaftesbury was involved in a movement to put the Protestant Duke of Monmouth on the throne instead, and his activities led to imprisonment in the Tower of London and, eventually, exile to Holland, where he died in 1683. Associated as he was with Shaftesbury, Locke's position in England soon became precarious, and he fled to Holland himself soon after Shaftesbury did. These events clearly had an impact on the development of Locke's political philosophy, not only where his opposition to absolute power and defense of individual rights and resistance to tyranny were concerned, but also on his conception of religious toleration, which granted a very wide range of latitude for religious dissent but is also generally understood to have excluded Catholics from the right to toleration.

Locke again returned to England in 1689, after the Glorious Revolution succeeded in enthroning the Protestant monarchs William and Mary. It was not long before the three major works – the *Essay Concerning Human Understanding, Two Treatises of Government,* and *A Letter Concerning Toleration* – were published, though Locke had been working on them for years. Only with the *Essay* did Locke publicly acknowledge authorship, however, reluctant as he apparently was in the still delicate political climate of the immediate post-revolutionary period to be too blatantly associated with ideas as radical as those expressed in the *Letter* and *Two Treatises.* Nevertheless, he was active in politics for most of the remainder of his life, and was made Commissioner for Appeals and a Commissioner for Trade, the latter position involving him in the affairs of England's colonies.

In 1691 Locke moved to Essex and spent many years thereafter in the household of Sir Francis and Lady Masham, the latter of whom had long been a friend of Locke's, and was the daughter of the eminent Cambridge Platonist Ralph Cudworth (1617–88). He published several further works, including a *Second* and *Third Letter for Toleration* (in 1691 and 1692 respectively), *Some Thoughts on Education* (1693), and *The Reasonableness of Christianity* (1695). The last of these works evinces Locke's tendency toward a minimalist theology, advocating as it does a simplified conception of the essence of Christianity. The *Essay* too had evinced unconventional theological views, and their soundness was challenged by Edward Stillingfleet, the Bishop of Worcester, with whom Locke engaged in an ongoing public dispute. But there were more friendly intellectual exchanges too in his later years, for instance with the likes of the scientist William Molyneux, as well as with Isaac Newton, with whom Locke shared interests not only in science but also theology and biblical studies. Indeed, Locke's final years were devoted to writing a commentary on the epistles of St. Paul.

Locke died in 1704. He never married, nor, as far as we know, did he father any children. He was also, as we have seen, frequently on the move. He did, however, have many lasting friendships, and as has been mentioned, he found in some of them a means of supporting himself. All of this enabled him to live fairly comfortably and in a manner that provided him much leisure to think and write. His religious convictions were deep, idiosyncratic, unsentimental, decidedly Protestant, and staunchly anti-Catholic. He was somewhat introverted and of a highly sensitive temperament, but not given to excessive emotion or frivolity. He was extremely careful with his money, and known to be generous to poor people who were simply down on their luck, but contemptuous of those who were shiftless and dissolute. "To live," he once said, "is to be where and with whom one likes." It seems fair to say that the kind of independence which Locke defended so vigorously in the intellectual and political realms found a parallel in the independence with which he preferred to live his own life – an autonomy in thought and action exercised with a sober religiosity, moderation, and reasonableness.

LOCKE

General introductions to Locke's philosophy include John W. Yolton, *Locke: An Introduction* (Oxford: Blackwell, 1985), Nicholas Jolley, *Locke: his Philosophical Thought* (New York: Oxford University Press, 1999), Garrett Thomson, *On Locke* (Belmont, CA: Wadsworth, 2001), John Dunn, *Locke: A Very Short Introduction* (Oxford: Oxford University Press, 2003), and E. J. Lowe, *Locke* (London: Routledge, 2005). Vere Chappell, ed., *The Cambridge Companion to Locke* (Cambridge: Cambridge University Press, 1994) is a useful collection of essays introducing various aspects of Locke's thought. John W. Yolton, *A Locke Dictionary* (Oxford: Blackwell, 1993) contains short articles on all the main concepts in Locke's philosophy. C. B. Martin and D. M. Armstrong, eds., *Locke and Berkeley: A Collection of Critical Essays* (Garden City, NY: Anchor Books, 1968) is an older anthology, but still useful. Maurice Cranston, *John Locke: A Biography* (London: Longman, 1957) is the standard work on Locke's life. The statement from Locke cited above is quoted on p. 10 of Thomson's book.

Chapter Two

Locke in Context

The Scholastic tradition

The modern period in philosophy begins roughly in the seventeenth century, with precursors in the Renaissance and Reformation eras. Early modern philosophy is defined more than anything else by its rejection of the fundamental metaphysical and methodological assumptions of the medieval Scholastic tradition. This is no less true of Locke's work than it is of the work of Descartes or Thomas Hobbes (1588–1679); indeed, Locke's *Essay* simply cannot properly be understood without a basic grasp of the Scholastic concepts and methods he is attacking.

Scholasticism was the philosophical tradition associated with the "schools" or universities of the late Middle Ages. It would be far too crude to speak of it as if it comprised a single unified system of doctrine that was universally accepted in all of Europe throughout the medieval period, though this caricature is common. In fact there was a great diversity of opinion. But there were nevertheless several themes deriving mainly from Aristotelianism that came eventually to predominate. Aristotle (384–322 BC), of course, was with Plato (429–347 BC) one of the two greatest thinkers of ancient Greece. Various developments of Plato's thought, such as the version associated with St. Augustine (AD 354–430), dominated Western

9

philosophy until about the twelfth century, when Aristotle's works, many of which had for centuries been unavailable to scholars in Western Europe, were translated into Latin from the versions preserved in the Islamic world. The impact made by these newly accessible writings was enormous. Aristotle, who had been as much a scientist as he was a philosopher, had put together a system of thought unparalleled in scope and power, and many came to regard his views as the first word, and indeed perhaps the last word, on the subjects with which he dealt. So great was his influence that eventually he supplanted Plato and other philosophers of antiquity in prestige, and came to be referred to simply as "the Philosopher." The contributions of other thinkers were often regarded as having validity mainly to the extent to which they could be incorporated into a broadly Aristotelian worldview; and the task of reconciling Aristotelianism with the Christian theological doctrine that then prevailed became a pressing one. St. Thomas Aquinas (1225–74) was more responsible than anyone else for carrying out this synthesis of Aristotle both with the lasting contributions of other philosophers and with Christianity. Thomism, as St. Thomas's system is known, was accordingly one of the most important influences on the late Scholastic philosophers against whom thinkers like Descartes and Locke were reacting. It will be worthwhile, then, as a prolegomenon to our study of Locke, to examine some of the key ideas of Aquinas and the other Scholastics.

Perhaps the most crucial philosophical concept of the classical tradition that the Scholastics inherited from Plato and Aristotle is the concept of *form*. The form of a thing is its organizational structure, something irreducible to the sum of its parts, which gives it its distinctive properties and capacities. Even if a computer and a television set are composed of the same sorts of materials – plastic, steel, glass, etc. – they are different sorts of thing and perform different functions because those materials are organized in different ways. Form is not reducible to a mere configuration of physical parts, though. Consider the form of a triangle. No triangle existing in nature perfectly exemplifies triangularity, because any such triangle – whether drawn on a chalkboard, printed in a book, or whatever – is going to have certain flaws, such as the lack of perfectly straight sides. It is also going to have certain features, such as being of a certain specific size or color, which have nothing to do with the form of a triangle *per se*: even if any given triangle is going to be either red, or green, or black, or whatever, and is going to have a base of such-and-such a length, there is nothing about triangularity as such that requires any particular color or size. So triangularity is not identifiable with any physical feature of any particular triangle.

Another reason the form of a triangle cannot be identified with anything material is that there are certain truths about triangles, such as that their angles add up to 180 degrees, that are *necessary* truths in the sense that they could not possibly have been otherwise. Had things gone differently, you might have decided to read another book instead of this one, but no matter how different the world might have been, the angles of a triangle would never have added up to anything other than 180 degrees. But if the truth that the angles of a triangle must add up to 180 degrees is a necessary one, something true come what may, then it is true whether or not any particular physical triangles actually exist. And thus it cannot be a truth about something material. For the same reason, though, it cannot be about something existing only in the mind. The angles of a triangle add up to 180 degrees whether we want them to or not; this is something we discover, not something we invent, and it would remain true forever even if every human being were to die tomorrow. So triangularity and the truths about it must in some sense exist independently of any human mind.

It was for reasons like these that Plato and those influenced by him took the forms of things to be neither material nor mental, but to exist in some third kind of way, as abstract entities outside of time and space which can be grasped only by the intellect and not by the senses. Aristotle inherited the concept of form from Plato, but though he agreed that forms could not be identified with anything either physical or mental, he was reluctant to see a form as a kind of object existing in its own right. For Aristotle, a form exists in some sense only "in" the things it informs or gives structure to – not in the literal, physical sense in which a piece of food is in your stomach after you eat it or in which tea is in the water into which a teabag has been placed, but nevertheless in a sense which ties the forms more closely to the material world than Plato would have allowed.

Now it is in terms of the concept of form that the Aristotelian conception of *substance* must be understood. A substance is an independently existing thing, as opposed to the *attributes* of a substance, which do not exist apart from the substance which has them: for example, a green ball is a substance, but the greenness and roundness of the ball are not, since these attributes exist (for Aristotle anyway) only in the ball itself. And a material substance, on the Aristotelian view, is to be identified with a composite of form and matter. Neither the matter of the ball nor its form counts as a substance, a complete and independently existing thing; it is only the two together that counts as a substance. This view came to be known as *hylomorphism*, which derives from the Greek words for "matter" (*hyle*) and "form" (*morphe*). To understand a material substance, on this view, requires understanding its form and not just its material composition. In particular, it requires grasping its *substantial form*, those specific aspects of its organizational structure that make it the *kind* of substance it is. The greenness of a ball is not part of its substantial form because a ball would still be a ball whatever color it is; but its roundness is part of its substantial form, because it wouldn't truly be a ball at all if it were square or triangular instead of round.

In Aristotelian terminology, the distinctive form and matter of a thing are its *formal cause* and *material cause* respectively, where the causes of a thing are whatever elements play an irreducible role in accounting for it. Even to grasp a thing's formal and material causes does not suffice for a full understanding of it, however. We also need to consider its *final cause*, which is what the thing is *for* – the end, function, or purpose it serves – and its *efficient cause*, namely that which brought it into existence. Fully to understand a heart, for example, requires knowing not only its material composition and organizational structure, but also that it functions to pump blood and is brought into existence by certain biological processes, i.e. whatever genetic factors determine that certain cells will form into muscle tissue of the sort that constitutes a heart rather than the kind of tissue that constitutes a liver or pancreas. In general, complete explanation of a thing entails the specification of its four causes.

For the broader Scholastic tradition, though, even to specify the four causes of a thing is still at most a necessary but not yet a sufficient condition for a complete explanation of it. The immediate causes of a thing are typically only the end-products of a series of causes. A ball comes into existence because the person who made it gave to a certain piece of matter the relevant form. But what explains the existence of that person himself? The heart has the end or purpose of pumping blood, but why is it directed to that end rather than toward some other end, or toward no end at all? Only if we can answer all such questions will we have fully accounted for the phenomena we started out trying to explain.

Here we need to take note of another Scholastic distinction, between *act* and *potency*. Among the features that distinguish the rubber that is used to make the ball is that it has the *potential* to be a ball – to take on a spherical shape, to be the sort of thing that will bounce, and so forth – even before it is made into a ball. This differentiates it from water, say, or smoke or shaving cream, none of which can be made into functioning balls of the sort a child might play with. The potencies of a thing, then, are its potentialities or powers, and its having the unique potencies it does is part of what distinguishes it from other things. By itself, though, the rubber of the ball cannot actualize its potential as a ball: it is, in the Scholastic terminology, a ball *in potency* (or potentially) but not *in act* (or in actuality). For it to actualize this potential, something outside it – a machine or a person, say – has to form it into a ball. But then, whatever it is that actualizes this potential in the rubber, if it is itself realizing some potential of its own, must have been made to do so by something outside of *it* – and the same thing must be said for anything that in turn actualized *that* thing's potential.

An explanation of a thing in terms of its efficient causes is inevitably going to generate a regress, then, and only if we can somehow terminate this regress are we going to arrive at a complete explanation of whatever it is we started out trying to explain – a ball, for example. Here we have the ingredients for one of the prominent Scholastic arguments for the existence of God, namely the second of Aquinas's famous Five Ways; and that argument crucially depends on yet another distinction, between *per se* (or essentially ordered) and *per accidens* (or accidentally ordered) causal series. A causal series *per accidens* can be illustrated by a man who begets a son, who in turn begets a son of his own, who in turn begets another, and so on. In this sort of series, each member is independent in the sense that it is capable of doing its causal work on its own: once he has come into existence, a son can beget a son of his own without the continued existence of his own father. A *per se* causal series can be illustrated by a hand which pushes a stick which in turn pushes a stone. In this sort of series, each member is dependent on the ones higher up in the series: the stone cannot move at all unless it is pushed by the stick and the stick cannot move, much less move the stone, unless it is pushed by the hand. Indeed, it is strictly speaking only the hand which is moving anything; the stick is merely an instrument of the hand, used by it to move the rock in an indirect way. Now the first, *per accidens* sort of series, which is one we usually think of as extending forward and backward in time, is one that Aquinas concedes might in principle be infinite: since each member of the series can do its causal work on its own, without the assistance of any earlier member, there is no need to trace the series back to a first member who is using the other members as instruments. But a *per se* causal series, wherein the members paradigmatically exist simultaneously – the stone's motion exists only when the stick's motion does, and its motion exists only when the hand is moving it – cannot in principle be infinite: since it is really only the first member of the series who is strictly doing any causing, and using the other members as instruments, such a series would not exist in the first place if there were no first member. With a *per se* causal series, then, if we know it exists at all we know that it must terminate in a first cause.

But any material substance is part of a *per se* series of causes as well as a *per accidens* series. For example, a ball depends not only on the series of historical events that led to its existence – the operation of a ball-making machine, the persons who made that machine, and so on – but also on certain factors present here and now and at any moment at which it exists at all, such as the state of its molecules, which depends on the state of its atoms, which depends in turn on the state of the subatomic particles that make up those atoms, and so forth. Even if one were to concede that the universe had no beginning, then, it would not follow in Aquinas's view that there is no first cause, for even a beginningless universe depends at *every* instant of its existence on various *per se* causal series, and *these must* trace back to a first cause. The first cause that Aquinas and other medieval philosophers were interested in proving the existence of is, then, not the deistic sort of God who "got the ball rolling" at some point in the distant past but may well have ignored his creation from then on. He is rather a God who continually maintains the universe in being from instant to instant, and apart from whom it would simply blink out of existence; for without such a being at the start of the set of simultaneous *per se* causes that govern the universe at every moment of its existence, those causes, and thus the universe itself, would not exist at all.

Given the act/potency distinction, Aquinas concluded that the first cause of the universe must be *pure act*, a purely actual being devoid of any potentiality whatsoever, for any being containing potentiality would be capable of being changed by something outside itself and thus could not be a *first* cause in the relevant sense, namely a cause underlying all other causes in a *per se* causal series. And as pure act, the first cause must have the various divine attributes: he must have *unity* – there can be only one first cause – because distinguishing more than one first cause would require appealing to some potentiality that one first cause has and another lacks, and a first cause cannot have potentiality; he must be *eternal*, existing outside of time and space, because to exist in time and space entails being capable of change, and thus potentiality, which, again, a first cause cannot have; he must be *perfect*, because imperfection entails some unrealized potentiality, and a first cause has no unrealized potentiality; and so forth. In short, the first cause of the world must have all the attributes definitive of God as traditionally conceived in the monotheistic religions.

That this includes those attributes definitive of a personal God, as opposed to an impersonal absolute, is most evident from

Aquinas's Fifth Way, which takes as its starting point the existence of final causes rather than efficient causes. For something genuinely to be directed toward some end or purpose requires that there be a mind that directs it toward that end. There is a conceptual connection between ends or purposes on the one hand and directing intelligence on the other. (Note that this claim is not contradicted by Darwinism, which holds, *not* that there are ends or purposes that were put in nature by the impersonal process of evolution rather than by a personal God, but rather that strictly speaking there *are no* ends or purposes in nature at all; Darwinism does not give an alternative explanation of what Aquinas was trying to explain, but rather denies the existence of what he was trying to explain.) If natural objects like biological organs genuinely have ends or purposes, then there must be an intelligence which directs them to those ends. The first cause of the universe, insofar as he is the cause of a world that contains ends and purposes, must accordingly be a personal God.

This general metaphysical picture had dramatic implications for questions about human nature. Like any material substance, a human being has a substantial form; and in fact, the soul of any living thing, including a human being, was on the hylomorphic view nothing other than the substantial form of its body. Now for a thing to perish, on this account, is just for its matter to lose its form, and therefore for a living thing to perish is, by definition, just for its body to lose its soul. But forms themselves are incapable of perishing: the matter that makes up a particular triangle (a set of ink marks, say) might lose the form of a triangle (if it is partially erased) so that that particular triangle goes out of existence, but the *form* of a triangle cannot lose its form because it *is* a form. By the same token, the *soul*, being a kind of form, cannot go out of existence and in that sense has a kind of natural immortality.

Given the Aristotelian view that forms only exist "in" the things they inform, however, this immortality is, at least as described so far, not of a terribly interesting kind. Even if the form of triangularity continues on after a particular triangle is erased, *that* particular triangle is gone forever; what "continues" on is not a particular thing or substance but a mere abstraction, the form that that triangle shared with every other. So if the human soul were immortal merely in the sense that the form of a triangle is, that would be no guarantee of personal immortality. But in Aquinas's view, the human soul is unique among all forms in being *subsistent*, that is, existing as a particular thing and capable of continuing in existence as a particular even beyond the death of the body that it informs. When a particular human being John dies, it isn't just the form of humanness in general that continues on, as an abstraction, but the substantial form or soul of *John himself* that carries on as a particular thing. John himself doesn't quite survive, for a human person on this view is a composite of soul and body – and thus form and matter, like every other material thing according to hylomorphism – so that with the body absent, John himself cannot be said to exist. What survives is only a part of John, though the most important part. But should the matter of his body ever be re-informed by his soul, as Aquinas thought would occur via divine intervention at the resurrection of the dead at the last judgment, then John would once again exist.

The reason Aquinas thought the human soul had this unique status was because even while associated with the body, it did not in his view fully depend on the body for its operations in the way all other forms depend on the matter they inform for their efficacy. Among the capacities of the human soul is intellect, the power of abstract thought; and as we have seen, for Aquinas and other inheritors of the Platonic-Aristotelian tradition, when the intellect grasps the forms of things it does not grasp anything material. The forms have a kind of determinateness that all material things lack: any material representation of triangularity is always at best an approximation and contains imperfections, but triangularity as such is perfect. But a thought about triangularity, such as the thought that the angles of a triangle necessarily add up to 180 degrees, must have exactly the determinateness that triangularity itself has, otherwise it would not be *that* thought: when I think that a triangle's angles add up to 180 degrees, what I am thinking is precisely that a *triangle's* angles add up to *180* degrees, and not that something *approximating* a triangle has angles that *approximate* 180 degrees. If such thoughts are determinate, though, in a way that material things and processes cannot be, then it follows that they are not themselves material. And so the human soul, which is what gives us the capacity for rational thought, does not depend entirely on matter for its operation – and thus, in Aquinas's view, it does not depend on matter for its continued existence either.

Like other objects in nature, and especially living things, a human being on the Scholastic view not only has a substantial form but also exhibits various natural ends or purposes, and these ends or purposes together constitute the good for man. The ultimate end is eternal communion with God in the beatific vision, but there are various other subsidiary ends, and these ends are determined by the *essence* or *nature* a human being has by virtue of instantiating a certain kind of substantial form. Such ends include self-preservation, procreation, knowledge, and many other things, and the specific content of our moral duties is determined by these ends: what we are morally obliged to do is what promotes the realization of our natural ends or purposes, and what frustrates those ends or purposes is, being contrary to our nature and thus to what defines the good for us, forbidden. For Aquinas, the basic principle that good is to be pursued and evil to be avoided is self-evident; and a study of the ends or purposes inherent in our nature reveals what specifically constitutes the good for us. On this basis, an entire system of morality, the classical *natural law* ethics famously associated with the Thomistic tradition in particular and the medieval tradition in general, was constructed. Ultimately, of course, natural ends or purposes depended in Aquinas's view on a God who *directs* things to certain ends. But the specific content of those ends need not be determined by an appeal to God's commands. It suffices to observe nature itself, and to read off from it the ends or purposes inherent within it, which are there to be found by us whether or not we are aware of the God who put them there. To this extent, then, natural law reasoning is, on the Thomistic conception, largely (though not wholly) secular in nature.

Later Scholastic thinkers developed on the basis of this fundamental picture of natural law a doctrine of *natural rights*. Now, for

Aquinas himself, right or *jus* in a social context concerned the right ordering of a community, a matter of everyone carrying out his or her obligations relative to everyone else. "Right" was understood in an *objective* sense, as a feature of a social order; there was no question of "rights" in a *subjective* sense, i.e. as moral claims to things, inhering in individual subjects. One might say that it was a matter of right that a person got the wages that were due after a day's work, but one wouldn't speak of that person as "having *a* right" to the wages in the sense in which that expression is used today. Later Scholastic thinkers did adopt a conception of subjective rights, i.e. rights as moral claims inhering in subjects, as a corollary of natural law reasoning. If it is true that we have certain moral obligations that follow from our having various natural ends or purposes, then it is also true that we will not be able to fulfill those obligations unless certain preconditions are met. I cannot realize the natural ends and purposes concerning self-preservation, for example, if people are constantly threatening my life and health and stealing my property. If I am morally obliged to fulfill certain obligations, though, I must have a moral claim to whatever conditions are necessary for me to fulfill them; "ought" implies "can," so that I could not reasonably be obliged to do something if I did *not* have a claim to what was necessary in order to do it. If there is a natural law binding us as individuals, then, we must possess natural rights to the things we need in order to fulfill that law; otherwise the law would be of no effect.

As the allusions made above to Platonic and Aristotelian notions indicates, Scholastic philosophers tended to build on the ideas of the greatest of the ancient thinkers, and carefully to take into account also the work of those writers who came between those thinkers and themselves, rather than to start from scratch from first principles of their own devising. Contrary to a common misconception, this was not simply a matter of blind deference to authority, but rather followed from a certain understanding of the nature of rational inquiry. The knowledge and understanding of any individual human being, however intelligent, is always going to be limited in various significant ways. No one person is likely to have available all the evidence relevant to a certain philosophical problem, or to grasp all the difficulties facing various possible solutions or the myriad theoretical and practical implications those solutions might have. Fully to understand a system of ideas therefore requires time and experience, more time and experience than is available to any one thinker. Wise inquirers, on the view prevailing among medieval philosophers, will therefore seek to integrate their thinking into the intellectual tradition they have inherited rather than try to "reinvent the wheel" on their own. They will have a healthy respect for the authority of that tradition; not by mindlessly clinging to every element of it come what may, to be sure, but not arrogantly dismissing it either, even when it contains things they cannot at first glance fully comprehend. St. Augustine advised that one must "believe in order to understand," by which he meant, in part, that intellectual insight often only comes when one has carried out sustained reflection on some idea that one has first taken on trust, and could not have comprehended *ab initio*. We are all aware of how true this is in children, who are not capable of seeing the wisdom inherent in parental instruction until they become adults themselves. For the Scholastics, this is in many ways no less true of adults themselves, even those who are philosophers and scientists.

This sketch of the Scholastic tradition has been somewhat lengthy (though I should warn that it has also been, unavoidably, something of an oversimplification, hitting only some of the high spots and ignoring the nuances and varying interpretations of the ideas mentioned). I have devoted as much space to it as I have, though, because nothing less would serve as an appropriate introduction to the intellectual background against which Locke was reacting. Locke has many of the same aims as his Scholastic predecessors; for example, he wants on the one hand to demonstrate the existence of God and the possibility of personal immortality, and on the other to develop a theory of natural law and natural rights, and like many of the Scholastics he takes the former, theological task to be a necessary prolegomenon to the carrying out of the latter, moral-theoretic task. But he also wants to fulfill these aims in a radically different way, a way that decisively rejects the Scholastic conceptions of causation, substance, potency, essence, substantial forms, and natural ends and purposes, and also the Scholastic tendency to see rational inquiry as properly governed by an authoritative intellectual tradition. A proper understanding both of Locke's specific arguments and of the problems many of his critics have tried to pose for them cannot be had without grasping how Locke was trying to maintain a delicate balance between accepting some parts of the medieval inheritance while rejecting other, seemingly equally fundamental parts.

Early modern philosophy and science

Locke's reasons for trying to maintain such a balance cannot be understood without a basic grasp of the modern developments in philosophy and science that effectively ended the dominance of the Scholastic tradition and put European intellectual life on a radically new footing. Here too Locke's relationship to his predecessors is complex, involving the acceptance of some elements of their thought and the rejection of others.

Whatever the diversity that existed within the medieval tradition, that tradition had nevertheless been more or less united on many of the themes mentioned above, as well as in adhering to Catholicism as a common moral and religious worldview and in accepting the essential interrelatedness of philosophy and science on the one hand and theology on the other. This unity was shattered by the Renaissance and Reformation. The former emphasized humanism over theology, empirical science over philosophical speculation, and a return to the sources of pre-Christian antiquity shorn of the interpretative accretions in which they had, over the centuries, become embedded. The latter fragmented Christianity into myriad competing denominations, elevated the claims of faith over those of reason, and replaced the authority of the Church and tradition with that of the individual conscience. One result of all of this was a trend toward skepticism, for the increasingly bewildering variety of opinions and methods led many to wonder whether any particular opinion or method could be accepted with any confidence.

The work of Descartes was partly a reaction against the threat of skepticism. Famously, his method was to see how far skepticism could be pushed, devising the most powerful arguments against the possibility of knowledge that he could so that in ultimately refuting those arguments, as he sought to do, he could be sure to have attacked the skeptic's position at its strongest point. Thus Descartes argued that there was nothing in the testimony of his senses that could tell him whether or not he was awake or dreaming, for his experiences could be exactly the same in either case. Indeed, there was nothing in that testimony, according to Descartes, that could tell him even that the external material world, including his own body, truly existed at all; for it was possible that an omnipotent evil spirit was deceiving him, causing him to believe that he had a physical body that interacted with a physical world outside him, when in fact he was nothing more than a disembodied mind hallucinating the existence of these things.

So it is possible for one to doubt the existence of any material reality at all, in Descartes's view. But it is not possible to doubt one's own existence, for if I am even tempted to do so, I must exist in order to do the doubting: "I think, therefore I am." What I can know with absolute certainty, then, is in Descartes's view my own existence as a thinking thing, and if I am to know whether anything else exists – for example, my body, the material world in general, or God – I must be able to derive that knowledge from elements internal to my mind. Here Descartes appeals to the notion of *innate ideas*, concepts and truths in some sense built into the structure of the mind or at least knowable without any appeal to sensory experience. Chief among these for Descartes is the idea of God, an idea I have within me whether or not I can know that the external physical world is real. Yet given only this idea of God, Descartes argues, I can rationally infer that there must be something external to me which corresponds to it; that is, I can infer that God really does exist. For an analysis of the idea of God as the idea of a perfect being shows that he must really exist, otherwise he would be less than perfect; and it reveals too that nothing less than a perfect being himself could have put that idea in my mind.

(Here Descartes is appealing to some idiosyncratic versions of the traditional ontological and cosmological arguments for the existence of God.) Yet if God really does exist, then being perfect, he would not allow me to be utterly deceived, which I would be if I could not trust my senses when they tell me that a material world exists. So my senses must really be trustworthy after all, and so too for the same reason must the rational thought processes I use to build up, from my innate ideas together with the evidence of my senses, a system of philosophical and scientific knowledge. Skepticism is thereby refuted.

Descartes's approach to justifying our claims to knowledge also had implications for metaphysics. Since I can without any contradiction or incoherence conceive of a circumstance in which I exist as a thinking thing in the absence of any material world at all, including my own body (i.e. the circumstance where I am being deceived by an omnipotent evil spirit), it must be at least logically possible for me to exist without a body. What I am essentially, then, is just a thinking thing, and not a material thing at all: the mind, soul, or self is in Descartes's view a non-physical thinking substance. So whereas the Scholastics tended to see the soul as but an aspect of a person, the substantial form of the body, and not a complete substance in its own right, the Cartesian tradition sees it as just such a substance, and as a compete person too, to whom the body is not essential. Matter itself is also reinterpreted. No longer is it understood as that which instantiates form; rather it is defined in geometric terms as being essentially extended in space, characterized by such properties as shape, size, divisibility, and motion. For in Descartes's view, it is only these sorts of properties that continue throughout all the changes any particular material object might undergo. A hard, yellow, sweet, and fragrant piece of wax put near a fire will lose its solidity, color, taste, and odor, but it remains the same piece of wax. Such sensory qualities as texture, color, taste, and odor – that is, what came to be called *secondary qualities* by early modern thinkers – must not be essential to matter, then; only *primary qualities* like shape, size, divisibility, and motion are part of its essence, and these are, as it turns out, just those properties of physical substances that can be described and measured in precise mathematical terms. Substantial forms accordingly drop out of the analysis of matter just as they disappear from the modern conception of mind, for such forms were taken by the Scholastics to be irreducible, each distinct physical substance having its own substantial form and thus its own unique essence. On the Cartesian view, since extension and motion are the only essential qualities of any material thing, all material things have the same mathematically quantifiable essence.

This essence is in Descartes's view something I know through the intellect rather than through the senses, for what I apprehend through the senses is just a sequence of sensory impressions; it must therefore be the intellect which judges that these impressions are all impressions of some one material thing. And of course, whether a piece of wax or anything else really exists at all is something my senses cannot tell me, for they are too feeble to guarantee even that I am awake right now and not dreaming the various things I think I'm experiencing. Since it is in his view only via *a priori* reasoning proceeding from innate ideas that I can have genuine knowledge of anything's existence, and since his view is also that knowledge of the real natures of things derives from pure intellect rather than sensation, Descartes's epistemological position came to be referred to as *rationalism*. His metaphysical view that reality consists of two fundamental sorts of substance, namely thinking substance (or *res cogitans*, as he called it) and extended substance (or *res extensa*) is known as *Cartesian dualism* or *substance dualism*, and even those early modern philosophers who rejected his view of the mind as a non-physical substance tended to endorse some variation on his account of matter.

Emphasizing as it did the quantifiable properties of material things and rejecting the claim that substantial forms and secondary qualities formed any part of their essence, Descartes's view of matter was a *mechanical* one, on which all phenomena in the natural world could be accounted for in terms of nothing more than the motion of physical particles. This "Mechanical Philosophy," as it was called, thereby regarded physical reality as a kind of machine, rather than modeling it on organisms, as

Aristotelianism tended to do; and for that reason it abolished final causes or purposes no less than substantial forms from playing any role in the explanation of natural phenomena. The basic idea of the Mechanical Philosophy was developed by early modern thinkers in two directions. Given their account of the material world as essentially extended, Cartesians held that it is impossible for there to be space devoid of matter, and regarded matter as infinitely divisible. By contrast, *corpuscularians* like Gassendi took solidity to be no less essential to matter than extension, and therefore affirmed the reality of void space and of fundamental, indivisible physical particles (or "corpuscles"). In any event, the Mechanical Philosophy, which had been introduced into modern thought by Galileo, was given great momentum by Descartes, and by the time of Locke and Newton had become the dominant theoretical framework for early modern science.

Locke was not as exercised as Descartes was by the question of skepticism, but he wholeheartedly endorsed Descartes's fundamental commitment to reconstructing all knowledge on the basis of what the individual mind could discover for itself, and this led him to eschew the Scholastics' regard for authority and tradition. But the same intellectual anti-authoritarianism also played a role in leading him to reject Descartes's commitment to innate ideas, for this notion was in Locke's estimation too easily appropriated by those who might seek to stifle liberty of thought by alleging that their own favored opinions were simply hardwired into us and therefore unchallengeable. In other ways too, Locke adopted Descartes's positions only halfway: he agreed that mind could not be reduced to matter, but denied that we had any knowledge of the existence of immaterial substances; he affirmed that the existence of God could be proved, but via *a posteriori* argumentation rather than the *a priori* reasoning favored by Descartes; and he endorsed the Mechanical Philosophy, but in the corpuscularian form favored by Gassendi and his friend Robert Boyle rather than the Cartesian version.

In going just so far in Descartes's direction but no farther, Locke sought to avoid the other extreme metaphysical end in modern philosophy represented by the *materialism* of Hobbes, who held that human beings were composed of nothing but

LOCKE

matter in motion governed by the same mechanistic principles operative in the rest of the natural world, and who was often accused of atheism. It was in his moral and political philosophy, though, that Locke was to differ most sharply from Hobbes. The medieval Scholastic philosophers regarded society as our natural condition and government as a natural institution, but Hobbes, as a materialist who rejected formal and final causes, denies that these things are natural to us in the Scholastic Aristotelian sense. His view was that individuals in what he called the *state of nature* – our condition apart from the existence of society and government – are and can only be governed by naked self-interest, so that the state of nature is a state of war of "all against all," in which life is inevitably "solitary, poor, nasty, brutish, and short." To escape this intolerable situation, rational individuals will agree to a *social contract*, the terms of which are that everyone will agree to submit to the absolute power of a sovereign governing authority in return for that authority's protection. This power must be absolute, in Hobbes's view, because the point of entering into the social contract is to end the violent conflict inherent in the state of nature, and to divide power between various authorities would merely lead to a continuation of that conflict at a higher level, as a war between the authorities themselves.

Locke shares with Hobbes the idea that government is not natural to us and rests instead on a kind of contract, but he vehemently rejects the absolutist form of government Hobbes derived from this premise. In Locke's view the state of nature, though not governed by the positive laws of any governmental authority, is nevertheless governed by the natural law, and this law puts severe moral constraints on the power that any government which might legitimately come into existence can have over its citizens. Yet Locke's conception of natural law, though differing from Hobbes's, crucially differs too from the version defended by the Scholastics. Locke wants to defend natural rights against Hobbes and other absolutists without appealing to the natural ends and purposes central to the Thomistic understanding of natural law, partly because of his commitment to the Mechanical Philosophy and partly because of the inegalitarian tendency of at least some traditional natural law thinkers to regard political authority as naturally devolving on some members of society rather than others. Locke appeals not to any Aristotelian final causes inherent in human nature but rather to the idea that human beings are equals by virtue of their each being the creatures of the same God.

The Lockean project

I have said that the theme of freedom, independence, or autonomy is central to Locke's philosophical and political thought. In the contrasts between Locke's views and those of his Scholastic and modern predecessors we see how this is so, and also see more precisely how Locke understands freedom. He rejects the medieval emphasis on authority and tradition, but also opposes Cartesian rationalism, innate ideas, and the speculative metaphysics Descartes derived from them. All of these notions tended in his view to lead to an unreasonable dogmatism and to the stifling of individual freedom of thought. He held that modern scientific method, however modest its claims ought in his view to be, does provide us with some knowledge – so that the rejection of dogmatism needn't lead us to the opposite extreme of skepticism – and also with an intellectual discipline that should prevent us from being indiscriminate in forming our beliefs. He rejected too both the Scholastic natural law approach to ethics and politics and the Hobbesian tendency to see morality as a product of human convention, a tendency which leads, in Hobbes's thought anyway, to absolutism in politics. To appeal either to natural ends or human contracts as the source of our rights would in Locke's view threaten liberty. Yet, since the source of our rights is none other than God himself, liberty does not entail license. For Locke, freedom is always freedom within definite boundaries.

Of course, previous thinkers, including ancient and medieval ones, also spoke of freedom and the constraints that ought to go with it. But with Locke we see an emphasis on individual liberty in the public sphere that is not present in these earlier thinkers. A medieval philosopher like St. Augustine would have emphasized the idea that freedom is most importantly freedom from bondage to sin and vice, a kind of freedom that even a slave might possess and even a king might lack. In the political realm too there is a contrast between ancient and modern conceptions of liberty, famously noted by the political theorist Benjamin Constant (1767–1830). For the ancients, liberty was associated with citizenship and the ability to participate in public decision-making, but there was no connotation of the autonomous pursuit of one's own personal private ends, as there is on the modern understanding of liberty. It is this latter, modern notion of liberty which Locke is concerned to defend. Given Locke's view that this individual freedom ought to be exercised within certain moral constraints, we might, to borrow a phrase from Russell Kirk (1918–94), call it the ideal of "ordered liberty."

As we will see in the chapters to follow, many of the tensions in Locke's thought plausibly derive from his attempt to reconcile his favored conception of "liberty" with his favored conception of "order." Locke's rejection of Scholastic and Cartesian philosophical notions in the name of intellectual liberty arguably threatens to undermine the foundations of the epistemological, moral, and religious order he wanted to establish, while the theological claims central to his conception of political order appear to sit uncomfortably with the doctrine of religious liberty he is usually associated with. Lockeanism seems pulled in two directions: rightward, back toward the medieval tradition he rejected, with its more robust theology and communitarianism; and leftward, toward the hyper-individualism, secularism, and skepticism of the contemporary world. It is no wonder that contemporary liberals and conservatives alike frequently claim him as an intellectual ancestor – and also no wonder that, as I suggested in chapter 1, Locke's philosophy is as relevant to our situation today as it was to the time in which he wrote.

FURTHER READING

For an excellent brief account of the spirit and main themes of medieval philosophy, see C. F. J. Martin, *An Introduction to Medieval Philosophy* (Edinburgh: Edinburgh University Press, 1996). A much longer treatment of the period most relevant to the study of Locke is afforded by

Norman Kretzmann, Anthony Kenny, and Jan Pinborg, eds., *The Cambridge History of Later Medieval Philosophy* (Cambridge: Cambridge University Press, 1982). A. S. McGrade, ed., *The Cambridge Companion to Medieval Philosophy* (Cambridge: Cambridge University Press, 2003) is a useful collection of essays on various aspects of medieval thought, and Andrew S. Schoedinger, ed., *Readings in Medieval Philosophy* (Oxford: Oxford University Press, 1996) contains a representative sample of readings from the writings of medieval philosophers. Among general works on Locke, R. S. Woolhouse's *Locke* (Minneapolis: University of Minnesota Press, 1983) and Michael Ayers' two-volume study *Locke* (London: Routledge, 1991) provide the most helpful discussions of the particular Aristotelian and Scholastic ideas that Locke was most concerned to combat.

The early modern period in the history of philosophy, as well as relevant developments in modern science, are surveyed in the essays in Steven Nadler, ed., *A Companion to Early Modern Philosophy* (Oxford: Blackwell, 2002). Richard Francks, *Modern Philosophy: The Seventeenth and Eighteenth Centuries* (Montreal and Kingston: McGill-Queen's University Press, 2003) is a briefer survey. Also useful is Daniel Garber and Michael Ayers, eds., *The Cambridge History of Seventeenth-Century Philosophy* (Cambridge: Cambridge University Press, 1998), in two volumes. Roger Ariew and Eric Watkins, eds., *Modern Philosophy: An Anthology of Primary Sources* (Indianapolis: Hackett, 1998) is a good source of readings from the works of modern philosophers.

The *Routledge History of Philosophy* series also contains some useful volumes, in particular John Marenbon, ed., *Medieval Philosophy* (London: Routledge, 1998), G. H. R. Parkinson, ed., *The Renaissance and 17th Century Rationalism* (London: Routledge, 1993), and Stuart Brown, ed., *British Philosophy and the Age of Enlightenment* (London: Routledge, 1996).

Chapter Three

The Essay Concerning Human Understanding

Character of the work

Let us first acknowledge its shortcomings. Locke's *Essay* is generally admitted to be among the least thrilling of philosophical classics – dry, repetitive, and too long, by Locke's own admission. The prose is reasonably clear, but it lacks the wit and sparkle of Hume, the fire of Nietzsche, the spiritual pathos of Augustine, or the literary elegance of Plato. The non-specialist reader will certainly learn something from reading it, but is not likely to enjoy the experience much. More substantively, the book is sometimes conceptually imprecise in a way that has a significant impact on the ultimate defensibility of the arguments and positions presented within its pages, with crucial distinctions that should be obvious often going unmade.

Nevertheless, the book *is* a classic, not only of philosophy but also of English literature. Together with Descartes's writings it set the agenda for modern philosophy – and as I have indicated in previous chapters, its doctrines are in some form or other more likely to be endorsed by contemporary thinkers than are those of Descartes. It is the most important and influential exposition in the history of philosophy of an empiricist epistemology, the view that the elements of all human knowledge are derived ultimately from experience rather than pure reason. It has shaped the modern conception of the nature of scientific inquiry more than any other philosophical work. And in the course of developing these main themes, it presents novel concepts and arguments concerning such topics as the nature of language and the concept of personal identity that were dramatically to redirect their subsequent philosophical exploration. It is a work in metaphysics, philosophy of mind, philosophy of language, philosophy of religion, and even the foundations of ethics as much as it is a study in the theory of knowledge.

To be sure, Locke evinces a certain modesty in the aims he hopes to realize in the *Essay*. In a famous passage from the *Epistle to the Reader* with which he begins the book, Locke writes that:

> The commonwealth of learning, is not at this time without master-builders, whose mighty designs, in advancing the sciences, will leave lasting monuments to the admiration of posterity: But everyone must not hope to be a Boyle, or a Sydenham, and in an age that produces such masters, as the great Huygenius, and the incomparable Mr. Newton, with some other of that strain; 'tis ambition enough to be employed as an under-labourer in clearing ground a little, and removing some of the rubbish that stands in the way to knowledge. (pp. 10–11)

The reference to these contemporary scientists – Robert Boyle, Thomas Sydenham, Christian Huygens, and Isaac Newton – is meant to indicate that it is their work that Locke regards as the great achievement of the age, an achievement he does not aspire to match in the *Essay*. His ambition, or so he here implies, is only to remove some philosophical obstacles that might stand in the way of further scientific advance – in particular, as we know from the body of the work, the Scholastic and Cartesian ideas he thought presented a false picture of the nature of human knowledge, "rubbish" that must be cleared away before the edifice of science can be firmly established.

While clearing the ground for natural science is indeed one of the tasks of the *Essay*, though, it would be a mistake to think that it is the only task, or even the main task. Locke tells us in the same *Epistle to the Reader* that the initial impetus for writing the book was a conversation he had with five or six friends on a subject very remote from the nature of human understanding, a conversation that became deadlocked when the intellectual problems that had arisen in the course of it came to seem irresolvable:

> After we had a while puzzled ourselves, without coming any nearer a resolution of those doubts which perplexed us, it came into my thoughts, that we took a wrong course; and that, before we set ourselves upon inquires of that nature, it was necessary to examine our own abilities, and see what objects our understandings were, or were not fitted to deal with. (p. 8)

Locke's friend James Tyrell was present at this discussion, and recalled that the topics of conversation were "the principles of morality and revealed religion." Locke's original aim in writing the *Essay*, then, was to determine what precisely the limits of human knowledge are where morality and religion are concerned, so that investigation of these matters could proceed in a way that was likely to bear fruit. While there are many topics dealt with in the book other than ethical and theological ones – and indeed, even these topics, when they are dealt with, are often treated in a fairly general and sketchy manner – there can be no doubt that these matters were central to Locke's overall philosophical project. As we will see when we look at his *Second Treatise of Government* and *Letter Concerning Toleration*, the moral and theological conclusions of the *Essay* are crucial to Locke's political philosophy. In particular, the balance Locke tries to strike in the *Essay* between arguing for severe limits on our knowledge, while allowing that reason is at least capable of demonstrating God's existence and the basic principles of the moral law, underlies his project in the *Second Treatise* and *Letter* of providing theological foundations for his doctrines of natural law and natural rights while allowing for considerable toleration of diverse opinions in matters of religion.

What unites Locke's scientific, epistemological, moral, and theological concerns is, I have suggested, a keen interest in defending the independence of the individual in his judgments on these matters, where this independence is always to be governed by reason. The enemies of this independence targeted in the *Essay* are the Scholastic appeal to tradition and authority and the Cartesian appeal to innate ideas; the threat to reason that he is most concerned to neutralize is "enthusiasm," or the fanatical tendency to base controversial opinions, especially in religion, on subjective emotion or an unverifiable claim to divine inspiration. As he puts it in the book's dedication (to Thomas Herbert, Earl of Pembroke), Locke wants to defend the right of individuals to entertain novel ideas, against those who regard "the imputation of novelty [as] a terrible charge ... and can allow none to be right, but the received doctrines" (p. 3). But thinking, not feeling, is the mode of Locke's individualism, and he tells us (again in the *Epistle to the Reader*) that his *Essay* is intended as "the entertainment of those, who let loose their own thoughts" (p. 7). Locke cares little for the hostile opinion of any reader "who says or thinks only as he is directed by another"; but "if thou judgest [his work] for thyself," Locke says, "I know thou wilt judge candidly; and then I shall not be harmed or offended, whatever be thy censure" (p. 8).

The *Essay* is divided into four books, the first treating "Of Innate Notions," the second "Of Ideas," the third "Of Words," and the fourth "Of Knowledge and Opinion." As already indicated, many other topics are dealt with besides those named in the titles of the books. The work went through four editions during Locke's lifetime, some with substantial revisions.

Against innate notions

Locke is famous for holding that the human mind starts out as a *tabula rasa* or blank slate, a "white paper, void of all characters, without any ideas" (E 2.1.2). An "idea," in his notoriously expansive use of the term, is "whatsoever is the object of the understanding, when a man thinks ... whatever it is, which the mind can be employed about in thinking" (E 1.1.8). What he has in mind, as soon becomes clear to the reader of the *Essay*, seems to include just about anything that can be characterized as an object of introspection: thoughts, concepts, mental images, sense perceptions, bodily sensations, and so on. This raises all sorts of questions. Doesn't putting all of these things under the blanket label "ideas" crudely gloss over some very important distinctions between them? Indeed, might the differences not be more significant than the similarities? Or does Locke think that there is some core attribute that all of them have in common, and which justifies assimilating them? What does it mean exactly to say that ideas are the "objects" of the understanding? When I think about my car, isn't it precisely my car itself that is the object of my thoughts, rather than my "idea" of my car? After all, if someone asks me what I'm thinking about, my answer will be "I'm thinking about my car," not "I'm thinking about my idea of my car." However these questions are to be answered – and we'll return to them before long – Locke's view is that there are no ideas that are innate in us in the sense of being hardwired or built into the mind. All our ideas derive in one way or another from experience. This is the main reason why Locke is usually classified as an empiricist.

By experience, Locke does not mean merely our perceptions of the world outside us. There is also our awareness of the world within, of our minds themselves. Accordingly, Locke holds that all ideas derive either from *sensation*, the observation of external objects, or *reflection*, the observation of our internal mental operations (E 2.1.2). One immediate objection that is sometimes made at this point is that if all our knowledge derives ultimately from sensation and reflection, then the capacities for sensation and reflection themselves cannot be derived from experience, in which case Locke cannot coherently deny that there are innate ideas. But this objection is confused. Locke does not deny that we have many innate capacities and abilities, including of course the capacities for sensation and reflection. What he denies is that we have any of the things that serve as the objects of these particular capacities – especially concepts and propositions – in our minds before the capacities have a chance to operate. We may be born with the capacity to form the concept of a cat or to entertain the proposition that the cat is on the mat, but the concept and proposition themselves are not in any sense in us until we have had at least some experience.

Philosophers who believe in innate ideas are generally concerned with more interesting ideas and propositions than these, however. For example, basic principles of logic have sometimes been held to be innate, such as the principle of non-contradiction, which tells us that the same proposition cannot be both true and false. Mathematical and geometrical concepts and propositions are also commonly put forward as examples of innate ideas. All of these are paradigm cases of objective truths that are assented to universally. Some philosophers have even held that basic moral, metaphysical, or theological principles (such as knowledge of God's existence) are built into the structure of the human mind. Descartes wanted to use some of these purportedly innate ideas as a foundation for knowledge. Why does Locke, who certainly had an interest in providing a foundation for morality, religion, and knowledge in general, deny that there are any innate ideas, propositions, "principles," or "notions" of any sort? We have pointed out already that Locke was concerned that any appeal to innate ideas might be used to justify dogmatism and stifle free inquiry. But it is important to understand that this concern does not really constitute an argument against innate ideas. The fact that a claim might be used by some people to try to justify questionable behavior does not by itself show that the claim is false. So even if belief in innate ideas could be used by someone to justify an irrational dogmatism, that doesn't show that there are no innate ideas. Locke's worry may give him a reason to *hope* that the doctrine of innate ideas is false, but it doesn't give him a reason to think that it actually *is* false.

Such reasons are offered in book I of the *Essay*, though, which is primarily concerned with developing arguments against the doctrine of innate ideas. Locke objects that beliefs about morality vary too widely from culture to culture for any of them plausibly to be built into the structure of the human mind, and that "children and idiots" sometimes fail to grasp even the most elementary laws of logic, which should not be possible if these principles are innate. He also argues that most allegedly innate ideas are ideas we are not usually consciously aware of, but that it makes no sense to say that an idea is "in" the mind unless it is being consciously entertained. If the innatist's reply is to say that an innate idea is in the mind in the sense that the mind has the capacity to bring it to consciousness, this would make all ideas innate, since all of them are in principle capable of being brought to consciousness. But it is not plausible to suppose that the ideas associated with sensations of color and pain, for example, are innate.

As many commentators have noted, though, it isn't clear that a sophisticated believer in innate ideas would be troubled by Locke's arguments. For instance, the innatist could argue that claims about the diversity of moral beliefs are exaggerated: cultures might disagree about what constitutes murder and theft, for example, but rules against murder and theft themselves – the idea that at least *some* killing and some taking of other people's property is immoral – do seem universal. Innatists also often hold that it might take some considerable reflection for us to bring to mind and understand some of our innate ideas, that prejudice or moral corruption might keep some people from acknowledging what they know deep down to be true, and that in any event we should understand the claim that there are innate ideas as the claim that the normally functioning human mind has them built into it. So it is irrelevant whether everyone, including children and insane people, explicitly assent to them.

Even the claim that the innatist's view would, when followed out consistently, entail that all ideas are innate is not something every innatist would be troubled by. Descartes held that the ideas associated with sensations are in fact innate, for the physical objects that produce in us sensations of color, odor, taste, and the like are in themselves just collections of colorless, odorless, and tasteless particles, so that there is nothing in them that could be the source of these ideas. (As we will see, this is a line of argument that Locke cannot easily dismiss, given his own theory of perception.) Some innatists would even hold that there is a sense in which complex concepts like "carburetor" are innate, because the more simple concepts out of which they are constructed are innate.

Now Locke would reply that even if there are some moral or logical principles that are universally assented to, there is a far easier way to explain this universality than to suppose that such ideas are innate: we can imagine instead that human beings will tend to acquire similar ideas by virtue of having similar mental capacities, such as the capacity for abstraction from what they have experienced. For example, someone encountering several otherwise different triangular objects will come to attend selectively to their common triangularity and ignore their other features, and in this way acquire the idea of triangularity. Similar explanations can be given for all of our other ideas. Ultimately, Locke's main objection against innatism is not that it can be decisively refuted, but rather that an alternative empiricist account is available and should be preferred on grounds of simplicity and greater explanatory power. Book II of the *Essay* is devoted to developing such an account.

Even before considering that account, however, we should note that exactly what is in dispute between innatists and empiricists is not at all as clear as it might seem to be at first glance. We have seen that the innatist position is somewhat flexible, with its adherents significantly qualifying their claims in the face of criticism. Locke makes significant qualifications too, for while he denies that we have any innate *ideas*, he acknowledges that we do have not only such innate capacities as sensation, reflection, and other cognitive abilities, but also such "innate practical principles" and "natural tendencies" as "a desire of happiness, and an aversion to misery" (E 1.3.3). Locke wants to insist that human knowledge is not possible without experience, an idea that few today would deny. Innatists want to insist that human knowledge is not possible without some innate factor, and also that many human cognitive and practical capacities are part of our biological make-up, and cannot be accounted for entirely in terms of contingent cultural and historical environmental factors – a view that also has many prominent defenders today, including the linguist Noam Chomsky and theorists working within the scientific research program known as evolutionary psychology. There does not seem to be any obvious incompatibility between these ideas, and the disagreement between Locke and at least more subtle forms of innatism may therefore be more apparent than real.

Indeed, Immanuel Kant (1724–1804) is famous for his attempt to synthesize the empiricist emphasis on experience and the rationalist emphasis on innate cognitive faculties into a unified theory of knowledge.

Yet empiricists and rationalists needn't have waited for Kant to see how these elements of their views might be combined. Aquinas and other Aristotelian medieval philosophers were certainly familiar with the idea that "there is nothing in the intellect which is not first in the senses," as Aristotle put it. But they did not conclude from this that the origin of our concepts can be entirely explained in terms of processes like abstraction. As Peter Geach, a contemporary analytical Thomist, has argued, to attend selectively to a feature like triangularity (to use our earlier example), one first has to have the concept of triangularity, so that there is no coherent way to account for the origin of that concept in terms of abstraction. A medieval Scholastic philosopher dealing with the questions to which Locke and the innatists gave their (superficially) different answers might have appealed instead to the act/potency distinction described in the previous chapter: the potentiality for having any given concept is innate in us, but it will not be actualized until someone who already has the concept teaches it to us. This would seem to generate a regress – one concept-possessor's potentials actualized by another concept-possessor, whose own potentials are in turn actualized by yet another's, and so forth – but as another analytical Thomist, John Haldane, has pointed out, for anyone committed to the overall philosophical framework of Thomism, this would simply form the starting point of an argument for the existence of God as the initial concept-possessor, a "Prime Thinker." (Nor could Locke plausibly dismiss this as merely an ad hoc way of rescuing this approach from an otherwise serious difficulty; for as we will see later on, Locke himself endorses a proof for God's existence that rests precisely on the impossibility of a materialistic explanation of certain aspects of our minds.)

To be sure, Locke, like other early modern thinkers, was highly critical of the Scholastic appeal to powers and potentialities. As Molière put it in a famous example, Scholastic philosophers pretended to explain the tendency of opium to cause sleep by positing a "dormitive power" inherent in it, but since "dormitive" just means "sleep-producing," such an "explanation" amounts to a useless tautology. Yet as scholars of early modern philosophy now sometimes acknowledge, this "dormitive power" sort of explanation is by no means as empty as it was made out to be. Indeed, the claim that "opium causes sleep because it has a dormitive power" cannot be a mere tautology, since early modern philosophers themselves often denied, without contradicting themselves, that opium had any such power even though they didn't deny that it puts people to sleep. To be sure, talk of dormitive powers and the like isn't by itself a terribly informative explanation (though the Scholastics never claimed that to speak of such powers was all there was to explanation in the first place), but neither is it devoid of content. Its import is that it asserts that opium's putting people to sleep is not an accidental feature of this or that instance of opium, but is essential to opium as such. More would need to be said in order to give a fully satisfying account of why opium causes sleep, but to say this much is already to say something significant.

It is also worthwhile noting that some important modern scientific concepts have also been accused of being tautologies. For instance, Karl Popper famously argued that the idea of "the survival of the fittest" is a tautology, since "fitness" seems to be nothing more than a tendency to survive. More specific claims in evolutionary biology (e.g. "vertebrates evolved from non-vertebrates") have also sometimes been claimed to have the same problem. Now of course, modern biologists find these concepts extremely useful, and some philosophers have tried to show that when carefully analyzed, such claims can be shown not to be tautological. The point is just that we need to be very careful before dismissing a concept that plays a central role in a sophisticated body of theory. That it seems tautological doesn't entail that it really is, or that the theory of which it is a part is explanatorily useless.

As we have seen, both Locke and his innatist rivals are themselves quite willing to acknowledge some sense in which we have natural capacities and tendencies. We have also seen that they are unable to give a clear account of how their respective conceptions of these capacities and tendencies really differ from each other. This being the case, it is hardly obvious that the empiricist and rationalist theories of the origin of our concepts really constitute an advance over the medieval approach. Nor, as will become increasingly evident as we proceed, is this the only area in which the relationship between early modern and medieval philosophical worldviews is more complicated than it might at first appear.

The theory of ideas

We have noted already that Locke distinguishes between ideas originating in *sensation* and those originating in *reflection*. This is a distinction between sources of our ideas, albeit that both sources are kinds of experience. Locke wants not only to tell us in general terms where ideas come from, though, but also to catalogue what kinds of ideas there are, and to show specifically how each derives from experience. Here he distinguishes most fundamentally between *simple ideas* and *complex ideas*, where both simple and complex ideas can originate in either sensation or reflection. A simple idea is one that has no component ideas as parts, that "contains in it nothing but *one uniform appearance*, or conception of the mind" (E 2.2.1); while a complex idea is one composed of various simple ideas. Simple ideas are accordingly the most basic ideas, and as Jolley (1999) has suggested, one way to understand Locke's theory of ideas is on the model of the corpuscularian theory of matter: just as the properties of all material objects derive ultimately from various combinations of the basic particles out of which they are composed, so too do the features of all our ideas, even the most complex, derive ultimately from the simple ideas out of which they are compounded. The aim is to demonstrate that:

> All those sublime thoughts, which tower above the clouds, and reach as high as heaven itself, take their rise and footing here: in all that great extent wherein the mind wanders, in those remote

speculations, it may seem to be elevated with, it stirs not one jot beyond those ideas, which *sense* or *reflection*, have offered for its contemplation. (E 2.1.24)

An intuitive sense of what Locke has in mind by a simple idea is provided by his examples of the coldness and hardness of ice, the smell and whiteness of a lily, the taste of sugar, and the smell of a rose (E 2.2.1). But simple ideas can be divided into various classes. There are those that enter the mind through one sense only (such as our ideas of colors, sounds, tastes, and smells), and those that enter through more than one sense (such as our ideas of space, extension, figure, and motion), and there are those that enter through reflection only (such as our ideas of thinking and willing), and those that can enter through either sensation or reflection (such as our ideas of pleasure, pain, power, existence, and unity). In every case, though, the mind is passive with respect to simple ideas: it can neither generate a new one that was not already put into it by sensation or reflection, nor destroy one that has already been put into it (E 2.2.2). It is only by operating on the raw materials provided by simple ideas, thereby creating complex ones, that the mind can take an active role in determining its contents.

The mental operations by which the mind processes its simple ideas are three: combining several simple ideas into one compound one; relating and comparing various simple ideas without combining them into one; and abstracting them from other simple ideas with which they tend to be conjoined in ordinary experience (E 2.12.1). It is natural to think that it is really only the first of these operations that generates anything that might strictly be called a "complex idea." Indeed, while in the earlier editions of the *Essay* Locke assimilated the products of the latter two operations to the category of complex ideas, in the fourth edition he more or less acknowledged that it is only the first operation that generates truly complex ideas. Still, this does not affect his basic aim of showing that all our ideas can be accounted for by reference to the mind's operating on simple ideas originating in sensation and reflection.

Among the deliverances of these operations, Locke distinguishes between ideas of *modes, substances,* and *relations* (E 2.12.3). The idea of a substance is a combination of simple ideas that represent a distinct particular thing capable of subsisting by itself: the idea of a man, for example. The idea of a mode is the idea of something that cannot subsist by itself, such as gratitude, which might exist in a particular man who is grateful but does not exist apart from some grateful person or other. The idea of a relation is just the sort of idea we apply when judging that one man is taller than another, say, or identical to or different from some man we had seen earlier. Modes can in turn be distinguished into *simple modes,* or modes which constitute mere "variations, or combinations of the same simple idea, without the mixture of another" (E 2.12.5), such as the idea of a dozen instances of some one simple idea; and *mixed modes,* which comprise several distinct ideas – for example, beauty, which consists "of a certain composition of colour and figure, causing delight in the beholder" (ibid.). Finally, there are also of course the general or *abstract ideas* deriving from the process of abstraction: experience gives one ideas of many particular men, but by focusing attention on what is common to them and ignoring what differentiates them, the mind forms the abstract idea of man in general.

Into these categories, Locke hopes to put all the myriad particular ideas we have, including some philosophically contentious ones we will examine presently. There is one further aspect of Locke's general theory of ideas we need to take note of first, though, and that is Locke's apparent commitment to what is sometimes called *imagism,* the notion that every idea is ultimately to be understood as a kind of mental image. This seems to be the core notion uniting all the various mental phenomena he labels "ideas," and it is a natural position to adopt if one starts by emphasizing sensory experience as the source of many of our ideas: your idea of a certain man, for example, can come to seem to comprise the mental images you now have of the way he looked and sounded when you spoke to him in person. But it is also notoriously problematic.

One famous objection comes from George Berkeley (1685–1753), who held that Locke's account led to inconsistency.

For example, Locke says that "the *general* idea of a *triangle* ... must be neither oblique, nor rectangle, neither equilateral, equicrural, nor scalenon; but all and none of these at once" (E 4.7.9); yet no image can possibly be all of these things at once. Berkeley's own solution to this difficulty was not to give up imagism, but to give up general ideas. But many commentators have suggested, quite plausibly, that Berkeley was in any event just reading Locke uncharitably here. Though Locke's way of expressing it may have been clumsy, his actual view is, not that our general idea of a triangle itself contains inconsistent elements, but rather that it is indeterminate because it is an idea which must apply to various specific figures with incompatible features. It must stand for triangles that are oblique, rectangular, equilateral, equicrural, and scalenon; but since it cannot be all these things at once, it must be indefinite between them. To be sure, this indeterminacy might itself seem to be problematic: wouldn't any image of a triangle have to be, say, either equilateral or not? And if it is one of these, how can it represent triangles which are the other? But as E. J. Lowe (1995) has suggested, Locke could argue that just as a stick figure sketch of a man having perfectly straight lines for arms can represent a man who does not have perfectly straight arms, so too can an equilateral triangle, say, represent non-equilateral ones.

In any case, there are more serious problems with imagism. Consider that there is nothing about a stick figure *per se* that makes it represent men in general, as opposed to some particular man or some subclass of men – or as opposed to a scarecrow, or a mannequin, or a street map, or an airport runway, or innumerable other things. That it represents men in general or any particular man is only because we have a convention of using it for that purpose. But the same thing would seem to be true of any image: there is nothing in your image of a man *per se* that would seem to make it represent men in general, or a particular man, or a photograph or hologram of a man, or an actor playing a certain man, etc. And if we supposed that some second image could fix the meaning of your image – that is, an image which somehow portrayed your first image as an image of men in general – then the same problem would just arise again for that second image too, and for any further image you might think to appeal to in order to explain the meaning of any other. So it is hard to see how our ideas, especially the concepts we have of various kinds of thing, can be identified with mental images.

Another problem is that there are many things we have concepts of that it seems clearly impossible to form any image of, including those things we acquire ideas about through what Locke calls reflection, such as "*perception, thinking, doubting, believing, reasoning, knowing, willing,* and all the different actings of our own minds" (E 2.1.4). Certainly an image of a person sitting quietly with his chin on his hand and a serious look on his face (such as Rodin's Thinker, to borrow an example from Jolley) will not do the trick. For now the problem mentioned in the previous paragraph just reappears: what makes this an image of *thinking,* rather than merely an image of sitting quietly with one's hand on one's chin and a serious look, or an image of doubting, or an image of a statue? Moreover, this sort of move wouldn't even be remotely plausible for things like negations, conjunctions, conditionals, and disjunctions. How could the thought that *unicorns do not exist* be represented in an image? How could an image that portrayed rain and a wet dog, say, be the thought that *it is raining and the dog is wet* as opposed to the thought that *if it rains, then the dog will get wet* or the thought that *either it will rain or the dog will get wet?*

There is also the fact that a mental image is something *private,* existing only in the mind of the person who has it, while ideas cannot be private, at least if they are intended to include the concepts we grasp and the propositions we entertain. Two different people can have exactly the same concept and believe, disbelieve, or at least consider exactly the same proposition, but they cannot have exactly the same mental image, even if they can have similar ones. When two people learn the Pythagorean theorem, what they understand is one and the same geometrical truth. But when they form mental images of a triangle, they are forming two distinct images, one in the one person's mind and the other in the other person's. We will return to this point when we consider Locke's views on language.

Given the serious problems that imagism is generally agreed by philosophers to have, some commentators have tried to find a way of interpreting Locke's position so that he is not committed to it. But as Michael Ayers has argued in his magisterial study of the *Essay* (Ayers, 1991), the textual evidence for Locke's imagism is "conclusive," and the view is closely tied, as we shall see, to several of Locke's other positions, such as his skepticism about our ability to know the essences of things and his view that our notion of substance is irremediably obscure. Moreover, without imagism, the empiricist claim that our ideas derive in general from experience loses its intuitive force.

Even apart from the question of imagism, there are well-known difficulties with Locke's attempt to show that all our ideas derive from sensation and reflection. We have already noted, in the preceding section, an objection to his account of abstraction. There are also objections to his analyses of several specific and philosophically central notions, such as substance and identity. There is too the related question of whether his account of the nature of our ideas allows even for the possibility of having knowledge of the external physical world, or instead threatens us with a catastrophic skepticism.

Perception and the physical world

Let us consider the last of these issues first. Locke says that an idea is "whatsoever the mind perceives in itself or is the immediate object of perception, thought, or understanding" (E 2.8.8), and that the mind "knows not things immediately, but only by the intervention of the ideas it has of them" and "perceives nothing but its own ideas" (E 4.4.3). Now Locke uses the term "perception" in a very broad sense, as a synonym for "thinking in general" (E 2.9.1). But for that very reason it includes what we would today normally think of as perception, namely the conscious awareness of objects and events in the external environment (and by extension, of what is going on in our bodies). Given statements of the sort just quoted, Locke has traditionally been interpreted as advocating what has been variously described as a "representative theory" of perception or "indirect realism." This is the view that there is a real, external, physical world existing outside our minds (hence it is a version of realism), but that we are not directly aware of that world in perception, but only indirectly aware of it, our contact with it mediated by our direct awareness of our own subjective mental representations (hence it is an "indirect" or "representative" version of realism). Just as in watching a live broadcast of a State of the Union speech, you are really aware of the President of the United States, but only indirectly, through your direct awareness of an image on a television screen, so too in perception generally are we aware of external objects only through our direct awareness of our own ideas of them.

Among the arguments traditionally given for indirect realism, the most important concern phenomena like illusions, hallucinations, and the like on the one hand and the causal chains linking our minds to the objects they perceive on the other. It is possible to have a hallucination so realistic that it is indistinguishable from a veridical perceptual experience. If someone puts drugs into your coffee which cause a hallucination of rats crawling around on your bed, you might find the experience as realistic and convincing as it would be if there really were rats there. Now in this case a certain brain process, call it B, was presumably the immediate cause of your experience, and drugs in your system were the ultimate cause of that brain process, no doubt with other brain processes intervening. But if there really had been rats on your bed, then those rats would have been the ultimate cause of B. Light from the rats would have struck your retinas, setting up a chain of signals in the brain that would eventually trigger B, which in turn would generate the experience. The distal causes of your experience are different in each case (rats in the one case, drugs in the other) but the immediate cause (brain process B) is the same in both cases, which is why the experience feels the same in both cases. The argument this has suggested to defenders of indirect realism is this: since the immediate cause, brain process B, is the same in both cases, the immediate effect must be the same as well; but in the hallucination case, the immediate effect is not the direct awareness of any such external objects as rats, since there are no rats really present, but rather the direct awareness of a subjective mental representation of rats; and so, in the case where rats really are present, the immediate effect must also be the direct awareness of a subjective mental representation of rats (even though in this case, there really are rats out there in the physical world causing the experience). The objects of our experience are generally real, and exist independently of our minds, but we are only ever aware of them indirectly, through our direct awareness of our subjective mental representations. This is the lesson taught us by the causal chains that come between us and the things we perceive, and by the possibility of vivid hallucinations.

That these sorts of considerations underlie Locke's thinking about perception seems evident from his famous distinction between *primary and secondary qualities*. Recall that Locke endorses the corpuscularian theory of matter, according to which all physical objects are composed of particles moving through void space. On this view, the way one physical object influences another is ultimately through the mechanical interaction of basic particles or corpuscles. Perception too, then, must involve a chain of causation beginning with the motions of particles in the object perceived, continuing with the impact of particles on the sensory organs, and ending with the generation of an experience by the motions of the particles making up the neural structures of the brain. Now physical objects, existing independently of us as they do, have certain qualities that:

> are utterly inseparable from the body, in what estate soever it be; such as in all the alterations and changes it suffers, all the force can be used upon it, it constantly keeps; and such as sense constantly finds in every particle of matter, which has bulk enough to be perceived, and the mind finds inseparable from every particle of matter, though less than to make itself singly be perceived by the senses. (E 2.8.9)

These are a physical object's primary qualities, and they include solidity, extension, figure, motion, and number. The ideas we have of such qualities, says Locke, "resemble" the qualities themselves (E 2.8.15). But physical objects also have qualities "which in truth are nothing in the objects themselves, but powers to produce various sensations in us" (E 2.8.10), and these are what Locke calls secondary qualities. They include colors, sounds, tastes, smells, and the like, and our ideas of secondary qualities do not resemble anything existing in physical objects themselves. Primary qualities are "really in [physical objects] whether anyone's senses perceive them or no," but not secondary qualities, which "vanish and cease" when the mind is not perceiving them (E 2.8.17). (Locke also speaks of a third kind of qualities, namely powers physical objects have to produce changes in the ways other objects affect our senses, such as "the power in fire to produce a new colour, or consistency in wax or clay" (E 2.8.10), though these "tertiary qualities" receive less attention from him than the first two kinds.)

Locke's way of making the distinction is famously misleading. In speaking of primary qualities as those which are "really in" material things "whether anyone's senses perceive them or no," he seems to imply that there is no sense in which secondary qualities are in objects themselves. But this is clearly just a loose way of speaking, and "resemblance" or the lack of it is the key idea here. What Locke really means is that while both primary qualities and secondary qualities are really in physical objects, there is nothing in physical objects that at all resembles our ideas of redness, warmth, sweetness, loudness, and other secondary qualities, while there is something in them resembling our ideas of motion, solidity, number, and other primary qualities. Redness, for example, considered as a property of an apple, is really in the apple, though only as a power to produce in our minds a certain kind of subjective color sensation, where there is nothing in the apple at all resembling that color sensation itself, even though there is something in it resembling our idea of its solidity. In that sense, the "redness" (that is, the subjective *appearance* of the color) is in our minds, not in the apple, while the "solidity" (including something resembling its subjective appearance) is in the apple and not just in our minds. (Some have suggested that Locke's talk about the "resemblance" of our ideas of primary qualities to the qualities themselves is merely intended to indicate that we have a way of characterizing such qualities independently of their tendency to produce certain ideas in us, but do not have a way of characterizing secondary qualities apart from their tendency to produce certain other ideas in us. But even if this is part of what Locke has in mind, he also really intends to assert that there is a literal resemblance between our ideas of primary qualities and the qualities themselves, as indicated by the fact that he chose the term "resemblance" to describe the relationship. He also uses related terms like "image" and "likeness" to discuss the relationships some ideas have, and others lack, to the qualities that produce them (E 2.8.7).)

The primary/secondary quality distinction is one that had been made earlier by Galileo and Descartes, though less systematically, and it is central to Locke's rejection of the Scholastic Aristotelian understanding of scientific explanation in favor of the corpuscularian version of the Mechanical Philosophy. For the Scholastics, colors, sounds, tastes, and the like, as they appear to us in perception, are qualities no less inherent in physical objects than any other. But if such objects are ultimately composed of particles, Locke argues, these qualities must have a secondary status. If you divide a physical object into ever smaller parts, at some point the parts lose the appearance of the color, odor, taste, and so forth of the object you started out with; but they retain the appearance of having solidity, motion, figure, and the like (E 2.8.9). Nothing in the particles that constitute a physical object resembles our ideas of secondary qualities, while they do have properties resembling our ideas of primary qualities. Locke also defends the distinction by appealing to the perceptual relativity of certain properties. To a hand which has been soaking in hot water, a bucket of lukewarm water will feel cold, while to a hand which has been soaking in ice water, the same lukewarm water will feel hot (E 2.8.21). Yet the particles that constitute the water are in the same state in either case. "Heat" and "cold" may exist in the water as powers to produce these various sensations, then, but the subjective *feel* of heat and cold exist only in the mind. They are as subjective and mind-dependent as feelings of pain or nausea (E 2.8.18).

Now even though Locke holds that our ideas of primary qualities, unlike our ideas of secondary qualities, do resemble the qualities themselves, it is easy to see how this distinction naturally dovetails with an indirect realist theory of perception. In perceiving the redness of an apple, you directly perceive something – the subjective appearance of the redness – that exists only in your mind, even though it is caused by something outside you and which you do not directly observe, namely the secondary quality or power in the apple which generates this appearance. But then your perception of primary qualities would seem to be similar to this in at least one respect: what you directly perceive in perceiving the motion or solidity of the apple is also just a subjective appearance of these qualities, even though in this case that appearance does resemble the qualities in the apple that generate it. In perceiving any of the qualities of a physical object, then, it seems to follow that you never perceive them directly, but only indirectly via your direct awareness of your ideas of them. Given that, as we have already seen, Locke says that the mind "knows not things immediately, but only by the intervention of the ideas it has of them" and that it "perceives nothing but its own ideas," the plausibility of the traditional interpretation of his view as a kind of indirect realism seems hard to deny. Some recent commentators have suggested that this interpretation is nevertheless not forced upon us, and it is true that Locke does not overtly present his view as an indirect realist one, in the way that later empiricists would. But that is surely only because the dispute over indirect realism as an explicit, worked out position itself only arose later, as a reaction against thinkers like Locke who seemed implicitly to commit themselves to it. The view does seem pretty clearly to be lurking between the lines.

It should also be kept in mind that there are different ways of interpreting indirect realism, so that even to show that Locke is not committed to some particular version of the thesis would not necessarily be to show that he isn't committed to any version of it at all. For example, instead of the television analogy alluded to earlier, we might think in terms of seeing something through gauze, hearing it through earmuffs, or feeling it with gloves on. The first analogy naturally suggests that we are in some sense "looking at" our ideas themselves, that they and not external physical things are the objects of our experiences – a suggestion which Locke's claim that the mind "perceives nothing but its own ideas" seems to commit him to, but which many philosophers regard as implausible or even absurd. But the second kind of analogy suggests instead that while external physical things really are the objects of our perceptions, there is nevertheless something intervening between us and them. This much is surely implied by Locke's talk of our knowing things "by the intervention of our ideas." It might also be suggested by the primary/secondary quality distinction itself: just as gauze lets only some light through, or earmuffs let sound through but in a distorted manner, so too do our ideas let into our minds some information about the real nature of physical objects (e.g. what their primary qualities are like apart from our perceptions), but not other information (e.g. what their secondary qualities are really like). Finally, Locke's examples of sensory illusions might suggest this second sort of analogy too. Even when you're wearing gloves while holding an apple, it is the apple you are holding and not the gloves; still, you hold it only through the gloves, and the gloves significantly affect the way it feels. Similarly, even though it is really water you feel (and not your ideas of water) when you stick your hand in it, you feel it only through the ideas you have of it, which can vary significantly depending on what you'd been feeling a moment before, the state of your nervous system, and so forth.

It seems hard to deny, then, that Locke is committed to *some* version or other of indirect realism. One motivation for trying to find an alternative interpretation, though, is that indirect realism is often thought to entail *skepticism* about the existence of the external world. If our perceptions are always mediated by our ideas, how can we know for sure that there really is a physical world existing beyond them? How do we know that we are not in fact just constantly hallucinating, victims to a deception of the sort Descartes described in his famous example of the demon? But this objection seems overrated. For one thing, some philosophers would argue that we can show that knowledge of the external physical world is possible even if the starting point of our knowledge is the subjective realm of our own ideas. But even if such arguments did not succeed, it does not in fact seem to be the case that indirect realism threatens us with skepticism any more than any other theory of perception does. The reason why there is a philosophical question about how we can know whether the physical world outside our minds really exists derives from the possibility of extremely vivid hallucinations, or of our being deceived by a Cartesian demon or by mad scientists who hook our brains up to virtual reality supercomputers of the sort featured in the film *The Matrix*. If these things really are possible, they would seem to be possible on any theory of perception, not just indirect realism. If anything, indirect realism has an advantage over other theories in being able to explain why this skeptical problem can arise in the first place: such a problem is just what we should expect if our own ideas are all we are directly aware of.

However, that Locke's particular version of indirect realism poses a uniquely serious skeptical challenge might nevertheless follow from Berkeley's famous arguments to the effect that the distinction between primary and secondary qualities cannot successfully be made out. Berkeley says, for example, that perceptual relativity applies to our ideas of primary qualities no less than to our ideas of secondary ones: the same object might appear large from one distance and short from another; a coin might appear round from one point of view and elliptical from another; and so forth. He also argues that certain purportedly primary qualities cannot exist apart from certain purportedly secondary qualities: for example, it seems we cannot make sense of something having a particular shape without supposing that the expanse contained within the boundaries of that shape has a certain color. But the lesson Berkeley drew from such considerations was not that the Scholastics were right after all and that secondary qualities exist in physical objects in just the same manner that primary qualities do; rather, he went to the opposite extreme and concluded that our ideas of primary qualities were just as subjective and reflective of nothing outside our minds as are our ideas of secondary qualities. Indeed, his view was, notoriously, that there *is no* physical world outside our minds. Minds and their ideas are all that really exist, and an apple, say, is not a physical object existing on its own even when no one perceives it, but rather a collection of ideas, namely the ideas of redness, solidity, sweetness, roundness, and so forth. The reason Berkeley took this radical step is that he agrees with Locke that all we are ever directly aware of are our own experiences and that all our ideas must somehow derive from them, and concludes that we cannot so much as form the idea of something existing apart from experience. For an idea, Berkeley says, can never resemble anything but another idea; in particular, as something inherently mental, it cannot coherently be said to resemble something whose nature is to exist apart from any mind and any experience of it. Yet since the idea of a material object is supposed to be the idea of something that does exist apart from experience, it follows that we can have no idea of such a thing. We cannot, in Berkeley's view, so much as *conceive* of the existence of a material world outside our minds. Nothing truly exists except relative to some perceiving mind, either our minds or God's. This is *idealism*, so-called because it makes ideas, in the empiricist sense, the touchstone of reality.

Now the reason Berkeley has no qualms about asserting the existence of other human minds, and of God – as opposed to concluding that he can have no coherent idea of *anything* other than his own mind existing – is that he holds that we do have at least "notions" of ourselves *as* selves, spirits, or souls, and also of our volitions or acts of will as causes. We can therefore form a coherent conception of the existence of minds other than our own, and to explain the orderliness of our experiences, he argues, we need to posit the existence of God as the ultimate cause of our experiences. But as David Hume (1711–76) famously showed, on a consistently empiricist account of concept formation, it is not at all clear that we can form an idea of the self or of causation. We will return to the question of the self when we examine Locke's theory of personal identity; regarding causation, suffice it for now to note that as Hume argued, it is hard to see how on an empiricist view our notion of a putative causal relationship between A and B can ever be more than the idea of a regular correlation between A and B, with no essential or inherent metaphysical tie between them. All we ever strictly perceive is that A and B are "constantly conjoined," in the sense that when A occurs, B tends to follow. But to perceive this is not to perceive any "necessary connection" between A and B. Even our perception of our own volitions is in his view merely the perception that certain acts of will tend to be *followed by* certain bodily movements, without any awareness of something in the acts which could be said to *bring about* the movements. For all we can know, the objects and events we observe in the world around us are entirely "loose and separate"; it is only the mind which projects on to them a connection, as a result of its habitual tendency to expect one when perceiving the other.

This is quite a comedown from the robust conception of causation associated with the Aristotelian Scholastic tradition. On that tradition, to ask for the cause of something is fundamentally to ask for an explanation of it, and as we have seen, a full explanation was seen to consist of at least four components, namely Aristotle's four causes. Where series of causes are concerned, there was also the notion that some of these, namely the causes comprising a *per se* causal series, were so ordered that the connection between them was essential, and inevitably traceable to a necessarily existing First Cause. The world, according to this picture, is ultimately rational and intelligible through and through. But the empiricist tradition from Locke through Berkeley to Hume represents an ever more thorough abandonment of the ideal of complete explanation and a belief in the world's intelligibility. All of these thinkers endorse Descartes's view that the first-person point of view of the individual thinking subject is the starting point of all knowledge, but they reject his rationalist commitment to innate ideas and the primacy of intellect over sensation. In consequence, Berkeley concludes that we can have no knowledge or even conception of a world existing apart from perceiving selves, and Hume concludes that we can have no knowledge or clear conception even of the self. Furthermore, Hume's conclusions regarding causation, if accepted, notoriously challenge not only cosmological arguments for God's existence but also the possibility of inductive reasoning and the very idea of a law of nature, thereby threatening the foundations of scientific practice. What we take to be knowledge of objective necessities in the natural world is, on a

Humean view, really just knowledge of the habits of our own minds. Since Hume it has become a commonplace to note that empiricism, though from Locke's day to our own associated as a matter of sociological fact with a confident faith in modern science as a source of genuine knowledge, tends as a matter of philosophical or conceptual fact to lead to a corrosive skepticism.

To be sure, later philosophers influenced by these classical empiricists have resisted their more extreme conclusions, but they have done so precisely by abandoning a thoroughgoing empiricist account of concept formation, as well as the imagism that is inchoate in Locke and explicit in Berkeley and Hume. If Locke's indirect realism is not to collapse into either idealism or skepticism, then, it seems that the Lockean will need to look elsewhere than experience for a more adequate conception of matter and causation.

Substance, essence, and language

This conclusion is arguably reinforced by a consideration of Locke's famous account of substance. For the Scholastics, as noted in the previous chapter, a substance is a composite of matter and substantial form. But early modern thinkers tended to reject the notion of substantial forms for the reason mentioned earlier, that they dismissed Scholastic talk of powers and the like: appeal to them was regarded as vacuous, a mere re-description in other words of the very phenomenon that is purportedly being explained. To say that opium puts us to sleep because it is part of its substantial form that it has the ability to do so is, according to many early modern philosophers and scientists, to utter a pointless tautology. Locke endorses this abandonment of substantial forms, and proposes an alternative account of what it is for something to be a substance.

The traditional reading of Locke's account is as follows. Our idea of a substance of a particular kind is in part a complex idea comprising simple component ideas of several regularly co-occurring qualities. For example, our idea of gold is in part a compound of the ideas of yellowness, malleability, fusibility, and so forth, and of the qualities corresponding to these ideas as frequently instantiated together. But we also take it that such qualities do not exist all by themselves, independently of something which bears them. Our idea of a substance therefore includes also the idea of a "substratum" which underlies these qualities and holds them together (E 2.23.1). The idea of such a substratum is also described by Locke as the "notion of pure substance in general" (E 2.23.2), and it is not to be understood as having any properties of its own distinct from those it underlies. For this reason it applies to every kind of substance without distinction, so that what differentiates various types of substances can only be the unique set of qualities that each possesses. The difference between a lump of gold and a piece of chocolate is that the former has yellowness, malleability, fusibility, and the like as its qualities, and the latter has brownness, sweetness, edibility, and so forth as its qualities; there is no inherent further difference in the natures of the substrata that underlie and hold together each of these sets of properties. A substratum can therefore be characterized at best as a "something," we "know not what," that unites the qualities of a substance (E 2.23.2). Our idea of substance in general is, accordingly, an "obscure and relative" one (E 2.23.3). It does not derive directly from experience, but is posited by the mind so as to make intelligible the regular co-occurrence of certain sets of qualities.

So understood, Locke's account has generally been regarded as seriously problematic. For one thing, it is hard to see how it can plausibly claim to be an improvement on the Scholastic account it is intended to replace. If the appeal to substantial forms is regarded as vacuous, how can the appeal to "something, we know not what" as an explanation of what holds the qualities of a substance together be considered any less vacuous? There is also the problem of reconciling it with Locke's empiricism. The idea of substratum or substance in general does not arise directly from sensation or reflection, since it is only ideas of the properties that a substratum is supposed to hold together that we derive from those sources. Nor is it a complex idea or derivable via abstraction, since to abstract away all ideas of particular kinds of qualities, which we would have to do so as to get to that which underlies them, would seem to leave us with nothing at all. If the mind really has such an idea, then, it seems it must have gotten it other than from experience. Berkeley and Hume, pushing as they did a more thoroughgoing empiricism, concluded that there just is no such idea, with Berkeley accordingly rejecting the very idea of material substances themselves and Hume the ideas of material and mental substances alike.

As with the traditional understanding of some of Locke's other doctrines, the difficulties inherent in this one have led some contemporary commentators to seek an alternative interpretation. To understand how this might go, we need first to consider another of Locke's key ideas, his account of essence, "the very being of anything, whereby it is, what it is" (E 3.3.15). Recall that for the Aristotelian Scholastic philosophers, the essence of a thing was to be identified with its substantial form, which like all forms was regarded as something existing objectively, entirely apart from human interests. Of course, for Aristotelians, this does not mean, as it did for Plato, that the forms exist totally independently of the material world, for they regard forms as existing, in general, somehow only "in" the things they inform. But forms are nevertheless considered irreducible to any set of material properties, and certainly to be independent of the human mind, which when it grasps them discovers something that it did not create. Locke rejects all of this, putting in its place a doctrine of essences more in harmony with his empiricism and corpuscularianism.

Here the key distinction Locke draws is between *real essence* and *nominal essence*. A nominal essence is a complex idea associated with a general term. The term "gold," for example, is associated with the complex idea of something yellow, malleable, fusible, and so forth, and that idea just is the nominal essence of gold (E 3.6.2). Nominal essences are determined by human agreement, and in particular by the conventions of linguistic usage. They are "the workmanship of the understanding" (E 3.3.13), reflective of human interests and historical accident, the contingent needs human beings have had for carving up the flux of the world around them in certain ways given certain circumstances. A real essence, however, is the "real internal ... constitution of things" (E 3.3.15), the nature it has independently of human interests. It is "that, on which all the properties of the species depend, and from which alone they all flow" (E 3.5.14), and indeed, is that "upon which depends [the] *nominal essence*, and all the properties of that sort" (E 3.6.2). Whereas yellowness, malleability, fusibility, and the like comprise the nominal essence of gold, "the *real essence* is the constitution of the insensible parts of that body, on which those qualities, and all the other properties of *gold* depend" (ibid.).

In the cases of modes and simple ideas, the nominal essence and real essence coincide. For example, the mode of triangularity is that of "a figure including a space between three lines," not only by virtue of the "abstract idea to which the general name is annexed" (i.e. the nominal essence), but also by virtue of its real essence, "the very *essentia*, or being, of the thing itself, that foundation from which all its properties flow, and to which they are all inseparably annexed" (E 3.3.18). But in the case of substances, the nominal essence and real essence differ. Anyone grasping the nominal essence of a triangle will thereby grasp its real essence, and can, by geometrical reasoning, discover its other properties. But to grasp the nominal essence of gold is not to grasp its real essence. To discover the latter, empirical scientific study is required. In particular, for Locke, to discover the real essence of a substance entails discovering its corpuscular structure, the precise arrangement of its fundamental particles that underlies and explains its primary and secondary qualities. The real essence of gold is not the yellowness and malleability we observe, but rather the inner organization of its corpuscles, unobserved and unobservable. Here we see enshrined what would become in the work of early modern thinkers and their successors a sharp cleavage between what Wilfrid Sellars famously called "the manifest image" and "the scientific image," and a proclivity to regard science as essentially in the business of stripping away the appearances of things to uncover a reality that is largely hidden to us in ordinary experience. The Aristotelian Scholastic tendency was to see the real nature of things as at least consistent with, and continuous with, common sense, albeit that the common man hadn't the deep insight into ultimate reality that was the preserve of the philosopher. But the modern attitude, by contrast, has tended to regard common sense as something likely to be overthrown by the advance of scientific knowledge.

Locke's theory of essences is tied not only to a theory of science, but also to a theory of classification and language. For the Scholastic philosophers, the forms of things, being objective, unchangeable, and mind-independent realities, determine an order of equally fixed and objective species into which all the various phenomena of our experience fall. These species more or less match up with the classifications embodied in ordinary language, so that careful definitions of terms and deductive reasoning from them can reveal the objective order of things. But for Locke, ordinary language describes only the nominal essences of things, which are mere creations of the human mind and do not correspond to real essences, identical in Locke's view to hidden corpuscular structures. Even real essences count as essences at all only relative to nominal essences: that such-and-such an inner constitution is the essence of anything is due merely to the fact that it happens to generate the properties that we, for our own purposes, have grouped together in a certain complex idea (E 3.6.6). So while various particular things might in their real essences "agree" or resemble each other in certain respects that will determine whether our classifications will be more or less useful for our purposes (E 3.6.36), these particulars are, strictly speaking, all that really exist objectively. There are no objective species in nature into which they can be neatly sorted. Species are an artifact of language, and are thereby a human creation: "the *species of things to us, are nothing but the ranking them under distinct names, according to the complex ideas in us*; and not according to precise, distinct, real essences in them" (E 3.6.8), and "they who make those abstract ideas, which are the nominal essences, do thereby make the species" (E 3.6.35). In short, whereas for the Scholastics species are objective features of the natural world having their ultimate source in God, for Locke "*the boundaries of the species ... are made by men*; since the essences of the species, distinguished by different names ... are of man's making" (E 3.6.37).

Locke's account has clear affinities to *nominalism*, the view that only particular things exist and that what particulars named by the name have in common is *merely* that they share that name – as opposed to the *realist* view that what particulars named by the same name have in common is instantiation of a universal or form, understood in either a Platonic or Aristotelian way. But Locke in fact thought that the particular things we classify into groups had at least one thing in common other than being called by the same name, namely that they had as their nominal essence the complex idea we form by abstraction from the particular members of the group we have encountered. Indeed, it is this nominal essence, considered as an idea, which the name associated with the group strictly refers to. For in Locke's view, "*words in their primary or immediate signification, stand for nothing, but the ideas in the mind of him that uses them*" (E 3.2.2). They are "external sensible signs, whereby those invisible ideas, which his thoughts are made up of, might be made known to others" (E 3.2.1), and someone will succeed in communicating his meaning when his words "excite the same ideas in the hearer, which he makes them stand for in speaking" (E 3.2.8). Of course, we ordinarily take the words we use to signify things rather than our ideas of things, and perhaps too to signify the ideas other people might have of things, but for Locke this is an error (E 3.2.4), although his talk of words' "primary or immediate signification" indicates that there is also a secondary and mediate signification to things themselves. In any event, since he takes universals to exist at least in the mind, as ideas or concepts formed by abstraction, Locke's view is sometimes called *conceptualism*, though this label is often regarded as denoting a minor variation on a view that is essentially nominalist in spirit.

Now, how is all this relevant to Locke's account of substance – the topic with which we began this section? In particular, why is it thought by some Locke scholars (the most prominent being Michael Ayers) to provide a way of interpreting that account so that it does not manifest the weaknesses that plague it on the traditional interpretation? The idea is this. As we have seen, Locke's aim in developing his account of essences is to replace the

Scholastic account, which he regards as obscure and methodologically misguided. So he is not likely to appeal to equally obscure notions if he intends this project to succeed. We have also seen that he takes the real essences of things to differ from their nominal essences, those complex ideas which describe the surface properties with which we are acquainted in experience. Only empirical investigation, and not common sense or *a priori* philosophical speculation, will reveal those real essences to us – if anything will, that is. It turns out, though, for reasons we will consider later, that on Locke's view not even scientific inquiry will reveal to us very much about the real essences of things. That the inner nature of gold, lead, and other physical substances conforms to the general corpuscularian model of the world is something he thought we had good reason to believe, but the specific details of that corpuscularian structure and the manner in which it generates the secondary qualities of objects are likely to remain forever unknown to us (E 4.3.13). It may well be, then, that when Locke evinces agnosticism about the nature of substance, he is really just expressing in other terms the same agnosticism about real essences that he defends elsewhere in the *Essay*. It is not that he is committed to some utterly mysterious and indescribable something-or-other that underlies and unites the qualities of an object – that which unites them is clear enough, being just the corpuscular structure that he thinks constitutes the inner nature of all physical things. It's just that the specific details of any given substance's corpuscular structure are something we cannot know.

Clever as this interpretation is, there are some significant problems with it. Arguably, it does not sit well with the most natural reading of Locke's remarks about substrata; and as several commentators have pointed out, if Locke really intended his account of substance to be understood in the light of his account of real essences, it is puzzling why he did not make this clear in the *Essay*, which nowhere asserts such a connection between them. It is also not clear that it really helps much to rescue Locke from the charge that his account is subject to the same objections he raises against his Scholastic rivals. To say that what accounts for the properties of a thing is an inner corpuscular structure that we can never know is hardly *more* helpful as an explanation than an appeal to a thing's substantial form.

There are other problems too with Locke's account of essences, apart from the question of its relationship to his view of substance. In arguing for the superiority of that account over the traditional Aristotelian Scholastic position (which he does at length in Book III of the *Essay*), Locke suggests that the existence of such borderline cases as "monsters" and "changelings" – human beings who are, respectively, exceptionally deformed physically or severely deficient mentally – shows that there are no hard and fast species in nature (E 3.3.17). To deal with such examples, Aristotelians would either have to posit, in an ad hoc and implausible way, that each such creature belongs to a species of its own, or contradict their own theory by holding that such creatures instantiate no form or species at all. Locke also argues that in trying to resolve questions about how to classify such borderline cases, we have nothing to appeal to other than the observable qualities of things, and cannot appeal to their real inner essences, as the Scholastics assume; that such questions are in any event typically decided by convention; and that in this respect questions about how to classify natural objects are no different in principle from similar questions about human artifacts. Furthermore, he claims that contrary to the doctrine of substantial forms, there are no properties that are essential to any individual: Locke says, for example, that he could lose his memory, ability to reason, or any body part and he would still be the same man (E 3.6.4).

The problem with these arguments is that they all seem fairly obviously to beg the question against the Aristotelian Scholastic view of essences. In response to the first point, the Scholastic philosophers would simply have denied that the only way for their account to deal with "monsters," "changelings," and the like is either to assign them to ad hoc species of their own or deny that they belong to any species. The right answer, in their view, is just to say that those who are deformed or mentally retarded belong to the very same human species as the rest of us. True, due to bodily or psychological damage, such creatures do not instantiate the form of humanness as perfectly as normal human beings do, but that doesn't mean that they do not instantiate it at all. After all, the realist tradition, going back to Plato, has always regarded *every* material instantiation of a form as deficient to some extent or other; there is nothing particularly problematic about the sorts of cases Locke cites. A broken watch is still a watch, and Da Vinci's *The Last Supper* is still a painting of the Last Supper despite the severe wear it has suffered. Similarly, even such bizarrely deformed human beings as John Merrick, the famous "elephant man," are still human beings for all that. For similar reasons, Locke's assertion that no property is essential to any individual is also question-begging. For the Aristotelian Scholastic tradition, the form of a human being is that of a rational animal; that is to say, an animal that has as part of its essence a potential for reason, which other animals do not have. So that a human being loses his or her reason, or never manifests it in the first place, does not show that reason is not essential to human beings, but only that some human beings who, by their nature, have reason "in potency" do not have it "in act." Moreover, Locke's claim that we have no epistemic access to the real essences of things simply assumes his empiricist theory of knowledge, and thereby merely denies, without disproving, the Scholastic view.

Finally, there are some well-known difficulties with the account of language associated with Locke's theory of essences. The nominalism, or at least conceptualism, inherent in his view does not sit well with his acknowledgment that there are at least some objective or mind-independent cases of "agreement" or resemblance between particulars, for resemblance is itself a universal. Moreover, when two or more particulars "agree" or resemble each other, they must do so by virtue of having some property or other in common, and these properties themselves would thereby seem to be universals. All of this conflicts with his official view that only particulars exist. There is also the famous and influential objection to the Lockean conception of meaning associated with Gottlob Frege (1848–1925), which many philosophers regard as decisive: if the meanings of our words were identical to subjective entities like ideas, accessible only from within the first-person point of view of the person who has them, then communication would be impossible; for there would in that case be no way in principle to know whether the meaning you attached to the words you use is the same as the meaning I attach to the words I use. Indeed, it seems that the meanings *couldn't* be the same, for your meaning would be the particular idea existing in your mind, and mine would be the different idea existing in mine. (And if Locke were to suggest in reply that maybe your idea and mine were both instances of the same type or universal, then he would once again be contradicting the nominalism or conceptualism that is supposed to be his official view.)

To be sure, all of these objections to Locke's account of substance, essence, and language raise many issues in metaphysics and the philosophy of language that philosophers have debated for centuries, and some of these debates continue to this day. It is possible that Lockean positions on these matters might yet be defensible. But Locke's own arguments seem to be seriously problematic. For this reason, some contemporary commentators on Locke have tended to adopt the view that the right way to interpret Locke's critique of Scholasticism – not only where questions of substance, essence, classification, and language are concerned, but also where he addresses the other issues we've been looking at, such as the source of our ideas, the primary/secondary quality distinction, and the nature of scientific inquiry – is not as an attempt decisively to establish the truth of his overall system of thought, but rather as a more modest project of developing an alternative to Scholasticism that might be said to provide at least a better explanation, on the whole, of the phenomena both worldviews seek to account for. Locke's aim, on this interpretation, is to merely provide evidence of greater plausibility, rather than knock-down proof or anything close to it.

We will want to look more carefully at this way of interpreting Locke, but before doing so, let us examine the remaining major arguments of the *Essay*. We will see that, whereas the views considered in the preceding sections reflect Locke's undiluted antagonism toward the Scholastic and rationalist traditions, some of the views we will look at next reflect a desire to preserve a certain degree of continuity with those traditions, albeit in a manner consistent with the Lockean themes developed thus far.

Personal identity

It may be that there is no other section of Locke's *Essay* that has been as influential on contemporary philosophy as his famous treatment of personal identity, which was in fact an addition to the second edition of the book. It is situated within a discussion of identity in general, part of the aim of which is to vindicate Locke's view that our idea of identity, like all other ideas, derives from experience, and to counter the Scholastic conception of identity. What is it that makes it the case that an entity remains the same entity over the course of time? In particular, what makes it the case that a person remains the same person over time, despite the sometimes radical physical or psychological changes that he or she can undergo? For the rationalists, identity is a clear example of an idea that must be innate. For the Scholastics, the identity of a human person is determined by his or her substantial form. Locke seeks an account of identity free of both these assumptions. His interest in the subject, though, is one the Scholastics and many rationalists shared: he wants to show that personal immortality, and in particular the resurrection at Judgment Day, is possible even if one rejects both Aristotelian substantial forms and Cartesian immaterial substances. For this reason, Locke says, an exploration of the topic of identity is no mere idle academic exercise (E 1.4.5). Nor is its theological relevance the only source of the topic's importance. As we will see in the next chapter, the nature of personal identity is also crucial to the moral and political issues Locke grappled with.

Locke holds that the criteria determining a thing's identity conditions are relative to the kind of thing it is or the idea under which it falls, "it being one thing to be the same *substance*, another the same *man*, and a third the same *person*, if *person*, *man*, and *substance*, are three names standing for three different *ideas*; for such as is the idea belonging to that name, such must be the *identity*" (E 2.27.7). A single atom is the same atom as long as it continues in existence; a collection of atoms is the same as long as every individual atom comprising it is the same, though if one atom should be added or one subtracted we are no longer left with the same collection; while in a living thing such variation in parts will not affect its identity as long as the collection of atoms composing it continues to be organized in the manner typical of the kind of living thing in question (E 2.27.3–5). This is as true of human beings as of any other living thing: someone existing at one time (as a child, say) and someone existing at another time (in old age, for example) are "the same *man*" or human being as long as the material components making up their bodies, however much they might vary over time, continuously exhibit the organization typical of a living human body (E 2.27.6).

As the quotation above indicates, though, Locke does not regard the identity conditions of a man or human being, considered merely as a certain kind of animal, to be the same as the identity conditions for a *person*. Locke defines a person as "a thinking intelligent being, that has reason and reflection, and can consider itself as itself, the same thinking thing in different times and places; which it does only by that consciousness, which is inseparable from thinking, and as it seems to me essential to it" (E 2.27.9). But it is possible, Locke says, for the same consciousness to be associated with different bodies. In a famous example, he says that the consciousness of a prince might come to inhabit the body of a cobbler and displace the cobbler's consciousness, so that the person in the cobbler's body would come to have all the memories of the prince's past life and no memories of the cobbler's life (E 2.27.15). In such a case, Locke says, we would say that the person now in the cobbler's body is really the prince, and not the cobbler at all. But in that case, sameness of human body is not essential to sameness of person: the same person (in this case the prince) might exist with or without a particular body (in this case with or without the prince's original body). For the same reason, personal identity is not tied to any other kind of physical substance. But perhaps more surprisingly, Locke holds that it is not tied to any kind of immaterial substance or soul (in Descartes's sense of the term "soul") either. The same consciousness might jump from one immaterial substance or soul to another just as well as from one body to another; for example, it is conceivable that your current consciousness might exist in the very immaterial substance or soul that once belonged to Socrates, with that substance having been wiped clean of Socrates' consciousness and memories and replaced by yours (E 2.27.14).

Of course, Locke is not seriously suggesting that such body- or soul-switching is likely ever to happen in the real world. His point is merely that since it is at least coherently imaginable, there is no conceptual connection between personal identity and identity of either soul or body. He also suggests that the possibility of such odd and puzzling scenarios shows that identity is by no means as clear and distinct an idea as, he thinks, it ought to be if it were really innate (E 1.4.4). In any event, where personal identity does in his view lie is in nothing other than sameness of consciousness itself: " 'tis [consciousness] that makes everyone to be what he calls *self*; and thereby distinguishes himself from all other thinking things; in this alone consists *personal identity* ... and as far as this consciousness can be extended backwards to any past action or thought, so far reaches the identity of that *person*" (E 2.27.9). As this last clause indicates, Locke's emphasis on consciousness obviously includes memories of certain past actions and thoughts as having been one's own, so that Locke is often described as holding to a "memory theory" of personal identity. But he also has in mind other states of consciousness connected to one another and extended continuously through time, so that contemporary theorists tend to prefer to label this sort of view a "psychological continuity" or "psychological connectedness" theory. The basic idea is that some person A is identical with some earlier person B just in case A's states of consciousness – memories, personality traits, and the like – are continuous with B's.

Clearly this account needs qualification, as is evidenced by the famous "brave officer" objection posed by Thomas Reid (1710–96). Imagine a brave officer who was flogged as a boy for stealing, captured an enemy standard during his first campaign in middle age, and in old age is made a general. Suppose that at the time he captures the standard, he could remember being flogged, and that as an elderly general he could no longer remember the flogging but could still remember capturing the standard. Locke's theory seems to have the implication that while the aged general is the same person as the middle-aged officer, and the middle-aged officer is the same person as the boy, the aged general is not the same person as the boy. But identity is what logicians call a transitive relation: if A is identical to B and B is identical to C, then A is identical to C. So Locke's account seems to reduce to absurdity. As philosophers inclined toward a Lockean view of personal identity have pointed out, however, this objection can easily be surmounted by relaxing the requirement that there be *direct* links of memory and the like between each stage of a person's life. If the aged general can remember being the younger officer, and the younger officer can remember being the boy, then there is at least an indirect connection between the consciousness of the aged general and that of the boy that suffices for continuity of consciousness and, thereby, for personal identity. A revised Lockean theory could therefore hold that A is the same person as B just in case either there is direct continuity of memories, personality traits, etc., between A and B or, if there is no such direct continuity, then A and B are indirectly linked by intermediate stages that are directly continuous.

However modified, a Lockean account of personal identity is clearly radically at odds with the sorts implicit in Cartesianism and Scholasticism, in a way that might seem to threaten the moral and theological assumptions Locke shared with his predecessors. For Descartes, the self is identical with a certain kind of substance, namely an immaterial substance or soul. This sort of substance has on Descartes's view a kind of natural immortality, so that a Cartesian account of personal identity allows for the possibility of rewards and punishments in the hereafter. But for Locke, the self is not identical with any kind of substance at all. For the Scholastics, on whose view the soul is not an immaterial substance but rather the substantial form of the body, a person is neither a soul by itself nor a body by itself but a composite of soul and body, and life after death is attained when the matter of a person's body is once again informed by the person's soul at the resurrection. But

Locke rejects this conception of the soul too, dismissing as he does the very idea of substantial forms. Yet Locke thinks he does have a way of defending the possibility of life after death, despite his abandonment of the Cartesian and Scholastic conceptions of persons: as long as God can create someone at the resurrection and Last Judgment who has your memories, personality traits, and the like, he will in Locke's view literally have re-created *you*, so that there will be someone who can justly be rewarded or punished for the deeds you perform in the course of your life. Getting one's just deserts in the hereafter requires only continuity of consciousness, and neither the Cartesian nor the Scholastic metaphysics of the soul. "Person," says Locke, is a "forensic term appropriating actions and their merit" (E 2.27.26), so that what matters in analyzing it is to capture our sense of moral and legal responsibility rather than any ontological subtleties. He claims to have accomplished that.

Nevertheless, there are still important respects in which the Lockean conception of persons has drastically different moral and theological implications from at least the traditional Scholastic conception. For the Scholastics, since a person's soul is just the substantial form of a particular human body, it is impossible for one person's soul to inhabit another person's body: anything that was really your body couldn't fail to have your soul, since it just wouldn't be *your* body if it didn't have the substantial form, and thus soul, of your body. Obviously, this rules out *a priori* the possibility of anything like Locke's prince and cobbler example. The essential connection between a body and its soul also entails that it just isn't possible for something to be a living human body at all without having a soul; for if it had no soul and thus no substantial form, it just wouldn't be a *living* human body. But a person, on the Scholastic view, is just a composite of soul and body; and thus it follows that every living human body is necessarily the body of a person. Here too Locke departs dramatically from the Scholastic view, since his view seems to entail that a human body utterly devoid of consciousness would *not* be a person. The radically divergent consequences of these two conceptions are if anything more obvious today than they were in Locke's time, for they lurk in the background of many of the fiercest contemporary moral and political disputes. Those who take a more or less Lockean view of personal identity are likely to defend the moral legitimacy of abortion and euthanasia, for they are more likely to take the view that fetuses and patients in "persistent vegetative states," lacking as they do the rich conscious lives of normal adults, do not count as persons. Contemporary natural law theorists, Roman Catholic and otherwise, are by contrast inclined to take the view that fetuses and PVS patients are persons precisely because they have living human bodies, and thus (given a broadly Scholastic metaphysics) souls, so that abortion and euthanasia cannot be allowed. On the Scholastic view, it is irrelevant that fetuses and PVS patients do not actualize their capacity to reason or have conscious thoughts, for what makes a person a person is the inherent capacity for these activities, and these creatures retain these capacities in potency if not in act. On a Lockean view, it seems, to persist in unconsciousness is just to cease to be a person at all. That is not to say that Locke himself would have endorsed the application of his views to a defense of abortion and euthanasia, which are topics he does not address, but it is to suggest that Locke's metaphysical views may have moral implications that he was unaware of. As we will see in the next chapter, Locke certainly intended that his defense of the possibility of life after death would help support certain moral and political conclusions he also wanted to defend. But it may be that other aspects of his theory of personal identity have implications that are less consistent with his political project.

Moreover, it isn't clear that his account really does succeed in showing that survival of death is possible. Suppose that at the Last Judgment, God creates not *one* person having all your memories and personality traits but *two* of them, A and B. Which one of them is really you? Locke's account would seem to entail that *both* of them are identical to you, since the consciousness of each of them is continuous with yours. But this raises again the problem of transitivity, since whether or not A and B are identical to you, they clearly cannot be identical to each other: if God decides after creating both of them to destroy B but leave A in existence, then surely the right thing to say is that one person has died and the other is still alive, not that the same one person is now both alive and dead. Consider also that even if God creates only one person having your thoughts and memories, this would still raise the question of why exactly we should consider that new person to be strictly *identical* to you, rather than being merely a perfect *replica* or *copy* of you. And if he or she is only a copy of you, then nothing God could do to that person would count as rewarding or punishing you, but rather as rewarding or punishing someone very similar to you for things you did. So it seems we need some further criterion of identity to avoid these "duplication" and "replication" problems – something which, when added to continuity of consciousness, will guarantee that it is really *you* that is resurrected at Judgment Day, not some mere copy of you, and also that one and only one person could possibly count as you. A Cartesian would appeal to sameness of immaterial substance, and a Scholastic would appeal to sameness of body, since on the Scholastic view, given that a human soul is the substantial form of a particular human body, there can be no possibility of more than one resurrected person having your soul. Now while Locke clearly dismisses the Cartesian solution, it might seem as if something like the Scholastic solution is open to him; for while he rejects the notion of substantial form, he does accept the general Christian idea that at the resurrection our bodies will be restored to us. But to appeal to the restoration of our bodies as essential to the *identity* of resurrected persons would be in effect to give up a Lockean view of personal identity, since it would be to concede that bodily continuity, and not psychological continuity alone, really does determine after all the identity of persons.

That a Lockean view seems destined to collapse into an amalgam of bodily and psychological criteria of personal identity is also indicated by another famous objection to Locke, associated with Bishop Joseph Butler (1692–1752). People sometimes seem to remember doing things they did not do, occasionally even things that were in fact done by someone else. So suppose I sincerely believed I could vividly remember drafting the Declaration of Independence. Would it follow that I am identical to the person who really did so, namely Thomas Jefferson? Obviously not: my "memories" would be bogus, a product of dementia or the like. So for a person A to have *apparent* memories of doing what B did is not enough to guarantee that A is really the same person as B; the memories must be *genuine*. But to say that A genuinely remembers doing what B did seems to presuppose that A really is identical with B. In that case, though, Locke's theory seems to be circular: it explains the identity of A and B in terms of A's having genuine memories of being B, and explains what makes the memories genuine in terms of the identity of A and B. To break out of the circle would seem to require appealing to what *caused* the memories in question: if they were caused by brain damage or drugs, they cannot guarantee personal identity, but if they were caused in a normal way – in the Jefferson example, by having been in a certain room in 1776 with a pen in one's hand, etc. – then they would plausibly guarantee identity. But such causal factors seem clearly to require the having of a body, so that rescuing a Lockean theory from this sort of objection seems once again to require abandoning purely psychological criteria.

Even this will not necessarily neutralize every possible objection, for certain puzzling scenarios seem possible even on a theory that combines bodily and psychological criteria. For example, we can imagine that the brain of a person with perfectly accurate memories is divided into two, after which each of the two halves are surgically transplanted into one of two bodies cloned from the body of the original person. Each new person is equally physically continuous with the original, and let us suppose that each also has exactly the same memories of being the original person. So it seems that the quasi-Lockean sort of theory we've been discussing would entail that each of them is the same person as the original person. Yet just as in the duplication scenario considered earlier, each new person in this "fission" scenario cannot be identical with the other new person, so that we seem once again to have violated the transitivity of identity. Some philosophers would try to deal with this problem by stipulating that personal identity is preserved by bodily and psychological continuity only when no such "branching" into two or more persons occurs, but this is notoriously *ad hoc*. Others, like Derek Parfit, have suggested that what such scenarios show is that, strictly speaking, there really are no such things as "persons" after all, at least not objectively. All that do exist objectively are certain bodily and psychological continuities and discontinuities. When these continuities are numerous and clear, we say that we are dealing with "the same person," and when they are few or unclear we don't know whether or not to say we are dealing with "the same person." But this reflects nothing more than an ambiguity in our use of the expression "person," which is a matter of convention. What counts as a person is determined by our interests, not by any objective facts.

This would seem to be a rather drastic conclusion to draw, but it is hard to see how it can be avoided once one abandons, as Locke does, both the Cartesian and Scholastic conceptions of the soul. Moreover, Locke's general account of essences, given its conventionalist spirit, would seem to entail a conventionalist view of persons in any event. Despite Locke's intention of reformulating the traditional Christian conception of personal identity in terms of a modern revisionist metaphysics, when the full implications of his approach are considered it may well constitute a radical departure from that conception.

Free will

Something similar might be true of Locke's account of free will, which is also motivated by a desire to preserve traditional Christian teaching within the context of an anti-Scholastic metaphysics and epistemology. Recall that the Scholastics, following Aristotle, held that to understand something requires knowing each of its four causes: formal, material, final, and efficient. This would include any particular human action, such as my typing this sentence. The material cause of that action would be the matter composing my fingers, hands, arms, and nervous system; and the efficient cause would be the set of neural events that leads to the motions of the muscles in my arms, hands, and fingers. But there is also the formal cause, which is the fact that the matter of my body instantiates a particular kind of substantial form – the human soul – rather than the sort of soul possessed by a plant or non-human animal, or the kind of form possessed by a machine or some other inanimate object. Lastly, there is the final cause, the end or purpose I had of expressing a certain thought.

Now in general, on the Scholastic view, one simply cannot have a complete explanation of anything in the physical world without grasping each of these four aspects of it, for they are distinct and irreducible. To understand what a heart is you need to understand not only that it is made out of a certain kind of muscle tissue and grew from certain cells, but also that it has a certain organizational structure and has the end or purpose of pumping blood. Similarly, to know that a certain action occurred in a creature composed of neurons, muscle tissue, and the like and was initiated by the firing of some of those neurons, cannot suffice to understand it; an appeal to its formal and final causes is also needed. Indeed, the most *important* thing to know in explaining a particular action is its formal and final causes. After all, to understand what a heart is, it is more important to know that it is for pumping blood and has ventricles and the like than that it is to know that it is composed of muscle tissue and was generated from certain cells; for in principle it could have been made instead in a lab, and out of plastic and steel, as artificial hearts are. In the same way, what is most crucial to understanding a human action is that it was done for a certain end by a creature with a certain kind of substantial form, a human soul with its distinctive capacities or powers.

Taking all of this into account would, for the Scholastics, be a necessary prerequisite to any meaningful discussion of free will. For the will is just a capacity, power, or faculty of the soul consciously to initiate action with a certain end in view. A free will is one able to evaluate those ends in the light of reason rather than being pushed in their direction by instinct, and this is something of which only a rational creature, such as one having a human soul, is capable. A free action, in turn, is one that actually flows from rational deliberation and is not determined by the causal influence of anything else in the created order. It is, you might say, a piece of behavior instantiating the form of a rational action rather than the form of a mere bodily movement; and for that reason it is to be understood as the kind of behavior characteristic of a creature having the form of a human being, as opposed to the kind of behavior characteristic of something having a very different kind of form, like a spider or a vending machine.

The early modern philosophers, as we have seen, rejected the very notions of formal and final causation, opting for explanations that appeal only to material and efficient causes. This entailed rejecting too the idea of the soul as the form of the human body, and the body itself was thus reinterpreted as nothing more than a collection of material particles governed by efficient causation. Finally, efficient causes were in turn understood in terms of the operation of deterministic physical laws. These ideas more or less created the problem of free will, at least as it is usually understood today: if human bodily movements are movements of physical particles according to deterministic causal laws, then it seems that everything we do is outside our control and we cannot be free. Descartes, of course, redefined the soul as an immaterial substance, and exempted it from the determinism that governed the material world; and since he took the soul to be the cause of at least some bodily movements, he partially exempted the human body from the network of deterministic physical causes. But since he too rejected the notion of formal causation, he could not appeal to it, as the Scholastics did, to elucidate the relationship between soul and body. Notoriously, this opened up a new mystery of how an immaterial substance could possibly get in (efficient) causal contact with a material one, and this "interaction problem" has always been the greatest difficulty for Cartesian dualism.

As we will see in a moment, Locke himself did not in any event quite endorse Descartes's conception of the mind. But he was certainly concerned to show that the problem of free will could be solved within the context of his empiricist philosophy, and for the same moral and theological reasons that motivated his theory of personal identity. The possibility of divine judgment requires not only that there be people at the resurrection who can coherently be said to be identical to us, but also that our actions in this life are free in a sense that entails that we are morally responsible for them (E 4.17.4). Locke's first move is to argue that talk of free *will* is, strictly speaking, unintelligible (E 2.21.25). The will is a power or ability of a person or agent, and since it is only a person or agent who can coherently be said to act, it is only his or her actions that can be either free or unfree. He then argues that freedom in this sense is perfectly consistent with determinism, adopting a "compatibilist" theory developed earlier by Hobbes. "*Liberty*," says Locke, is just "the power a man has to do or forbear doing any particular action, according as its doing or forbearance has the actual preference in the mind, which is the same thing as to say, according as he himself *wills* it" (E 2.21.15). On this view, so long as nothing keeps us from doing what we want to do, our actions are free. If I were to type this sentence because someone put a gun to my head and threatened to shoot if I did not, or moved my arm without my consent, then my typing would not count as a free action. But if I type simply because I feel like doing so, my action is free. Whether my wanting to type was itself determined by some causal factors outside my control is irrelevant.

A frequent objection to this sort of theory is that it fails to capture the intuition that for any of our actions genuinely to be free, it must be the case that we could have acted in some different way; for if our actions are determined, then we could not have failed to perform them. Indeed, Locke himself alludes to the idea that we "could have done otherwise" as a component of the idea of freedom (E 4.17.4), raising the question of whether his account is entirely consistent. It is possible, though, that what Locke has in mind here is just the standard compatibilist interpretation of the words "could have done otherwise," usually put forward in reply to the objection at hand, according to which I could have done otherwise than I did as long as nothing would have impeded me in doing what I wanted to do *if* I had wanted to do something different. In other words, as long as, had I wanted not to type, nothing would have forced me to type anyway, then we can say that I "could have done otherwise" than type; and this is true even if in fact my wanting to type was causally determined. Obviously, though, if my wanting to type was causally determined, then there is still a clear sense in which I could not have done otherwise, and critics of compatibilism would hold that *that* is the sense relevant to the question of whether we are truly free.

This is, of course, a long-standing philosophical dispute, and one that cannot be settled here. It is important to be clear, though, on how radically different Locke's compatibilist account of free action is from that of the Scholastic tradition he rejects, whether or not one thinks his account can be defended. For the Scholastics, the rational deliberation that guides our actions is utterly irreducible to the sorts of processes that determine events in the material world; or, to put the point in terms of contemporary philosophical parlance, the space of reasons is for them necessarily distinct from the space of causes. The former can only be understood in terms of formal and final causation, and not in terms of the sort of material and efficient causes that characterize the latter. But for Locke, as for other moderns who reject formal and final causation, the space of reasons tends to collapse into the space of causes. It is hard to see how, on this view, human actions can fail to be anything more than a special case of the sort of impersonal mechanistic causal processes that prevail elsewhere in the material world. Defenders of the view would say that unless our actions are determined by such processes, they will be mere random events, and that randomness is even less plausible a guarantor of the possibility of freedom than determinism is. But to assume that determinism and randomness are the only two possible ways of conceiving of human action merely presupposes that the Scholastic view is false, and does nothing to show that it is; for a third possibility – the possibility, as I have said, of conceiving of an agent's reasons for acting as the formal-cum-final causes of his or her behavior, rather than as a species of either determining efficient causes or random events – is precisely what that view offers. Whatever one thinks of this Scholastic approach, its abandonment closes off certain philosophical options that its adherents would quite understandably regard as crucial to the defense of free will.

As with the modern approach toward personal identity, the modern view of human action is part of a general trend in modern thought toward a "disenchantment" of the human world, a progressive abandonment of the notion that human beings have by their very nature a dignity that raises them above the rest of the material and animal realms. It is noteworthy that Locke, who definitely has an interest in preserving some elements of the older conception of human dignity, more or less completely endorses, and indeed contributes to, the general metaphysical picture of the world that underlies the standard attacks on that conception. As I have already suggested, this cannot fail to raise the question of whether he can have his cake and eat it too. We have looked at some reasons to doubt that this is entirely possible, and we will examine some others when we see, in the next chapter, what implications Locke's metaphysics and epistemology might have for his moral and political philosophy.

Thinking matter and the existence of God

There is one further area in which Locke famously attempts to defend some traditional theological claims while at least partially rejecting their traditional philosophical justification, and that is his argument from the nature of the human mind to the existence of God. The background to this argument is Locke's general account of the relationship between mind and body, the proper interpretation of which has been a matter of considerable debate. There are passages in the *Essay* which sound like defenses of Cartesian substance dualism. For example, Locke notes that just as we take physical properties to inhere in material substances rather than subsisting on their own, so too we tend to regard mental qualities like thinking and reasoning as inhering in spiritual substances; and he acknowledges that "*we have as clear a notion of the substance of spirit, as we have of body,*" so that the obscurity of our idea of substance in general is no more reason to doubt the existence of spiritual substances than it is reason to doubt the existence of physical substances (E 2.23.5). He says too that "seeing or hearing" not only reveal the existence of material things outside me, but even more certainly reveal "that there is some spiritual being within me, that sees and hears. This I must be convinced cannot be the action of bare insensible matter; nor ever could be without an immaterial thinking being" (E 2.23.15). On the other hand, Locke also famously holds that we are unable to know "whether any mere material being thinks, or no," for there is nothing in "the ideas of *matter* and *thinking*" that rules out that God might have "given to some systems of matter fitly disposed, a power to perceive and think" (E 4.3.6). "For I see no contradiction in it," Locke says, "that the first eternal thinking being, should, if he pleased, give to certain systems of created senseless matter, put together as he thinks fit, some degrees of sense, perception, and thought" (ibid.). This would seem to leave it open that materialism might be true after all; in any event, Bishop Stillingfleet and other contemporary critics of Locke feared that this was the implication of Locke's view.

Recent commentators tend to think that Locke does not in fact mean to endorse either Cartesian dualism or materialism, but is rather an agnostic concerning the nature of the substance underlying mental properties. This interpretation seems well supported by Locke's account of substance in general, and allows for a plausible harmonization of passages like those just quoted. Recall that on Locke's view, our idea of the substratum underlying a thing's properties is an obscure one, the notion of a "something, we know not what" that holds the properties together. If this really is all there is to the idea, then it is reasonable to hold that we cannot know whether the "something" that underlies mental properties like thinking and perceiving is of the same or a different sort from the "something" that underlies material ones like motion and extension. There just isn't enough content to the notion of substance to allow us to judge one way or the other. Hence, we can say both that the dualist's notion of spiritual substance is every bit as clear as our notion of material substance – that is to say, not very clear at all – and also that for all we know a material substance might be capable of supporting mental properties. There might be two different kinds of substances here, but there might not be, and nothing in our idea of substance will allow us to decide whether it is the Cartesian dualist or the materialist who is correct. Even Locke's comment to the effect that there is a "spiritual being within me, that sees and hears" can be understood in a way consistent with this interpretation, insofar as Locke sometimes uses the expression "spiritual substance" to connote merely a substance which carries out paradigmatically "spiritual" operations like thinking and perceiving, which, on the interpretation in question, even a material substance might in principle be capable of.

But though this interpretation has much to be said for it, it is not the end of the story. For one thing, Locke does explicitly affirm that even if we cannot know for certain whether substance dualism is true, it is nevertheless "the more probable opinion" (E 2.27.25). Nor is this a view that must remain utterly ungrounded given Locke's agnosticism about the nature of substratum. For while his commitment to *substance* dualism is indeed ambiguous at best, his adherence to what contemporary philosophers call *property* dualism seems clear. Locke may doubt whether we can know, at least from an analysis of the concept of substance by itself, whether there are distinct mental and physical substances, but he is not at all doubtful that there really is an absolute metaphysical distinction between mental and physical properties. Thinking and perceiving, on his view, are simply not reducible to motions in the brain or any other such physical processes and attributes. Even if mental properties turned out to be properties of a material substance, then, they could not be identifiable with material properties of that substance. And if it seems mysterious how non-material properties could inhere in a material substance, this might give at least indirect and inconclusive support for the view that they inhere in an immaterial or spiritual substance after all – which may be the reason Locke held substance dualism to be "the more probable opinion."

Locke's property dualism is most evident from his argument for God's existence, of which it forms an essential component. Let us now turn to that argument itself, then, which is developed in the course of chapter 10 of book 4 of the *Essay*. The first stage of the argument tries to demonstrate the existence of an eternal being. We know that there are things in existence here and now; at the very least, Locke says, everyone knows for certain of his or her own existence (E 4.10.2). But we also know that something cannot come from nothing, or as Locke puts it, that "bare *nothing can no more produce any real being, than it can be equal to two right angles*"

(E 4.10.3). If anything now existing ever came into existence, then, something must have brought it into existence; and if whatever brought it into existence itself had a beginning, then that thing too must have been brought into existence, and so on and on. But then, "it is an evident demonstration, that from eternity there has been something; since what was not from eternity, had a beginning; and what had a beginning, must be produced by something else" (ibid.). That is to say, there must be a first cause of all things that have come into existence, an "eternal source of all being" (E 4.10.4). Next, Locke argues that this first cause must be the most powerful of all beings, for as the cause of all things that exist, it is also the cause of their individual powers and thus "the source and original of all power" (ibid.). Moreover, these powers include the powers of perceiving and knowing manifested in thinking creatures like ourselves, so that as the source of all perception and knowledge the eternal source of being must be the most knowing being (E 4.10.5). But "it is as repugnant to the idea of senseless matter, that it should put into itself sense, perception, and knowledge, as it is repugnant to the idea of a triangle, that it should put into itself greater angles than two right ones" (ibid.). Of itself, matter is in Locke's view simply incapable of generating mental properties, for "unthinking particles of matter, however put together, can have nothing thereby added to them, but a new relation of position, which 'tis impossible should give thought and knowledge to them" (E 4.10.16). Whatever the ultimate source of mental properties like perception and knowledge is, then, it must in Locke's view be something immaterial (E 4.10.14–16). This does not contradict Locke's earlier claim that certain "systems of matter fitly disposed" might be capable of thought, because he took this to be possible only if God were to "superadd" mental properties to such systems (E 4.3.6); he does not claim that they could ever exhibit such properties on their own. In any case, that the being whose existence Locke claims to have proved is indeed the God of traditional theism is taken by him to be sufficiently demonstrated by the fact that it is an immaterial eternal cause of the world that is the most powerful and knowing of beings.

Obviously, we have here an argument that cannot possibly be fully assessed without an extended excursus into the philosophy of mind, and in particular an examination of materialist arguments purporting to show that, contra Locke, it is possible for purely material systems to acquire mental properties via entirely natural processes. Equally obviously, this is a task that is far beyond the scope of the present book – though, for what it is worth, I have written another book which addresses these issues in detail, and in which I provide reasons for thinking that no such materialist arguments can succeed. I am inclined, then, to think that Locke was right to hold that it is impossible for material processes, all by themselves, ever to generate mental properties. Nor is this a view lacking in able and influential defenders among contemporary philosophers. It is, in any event, well motivated by Locke's own general philosophical commitments. As was pointed out by the Cambridge Platonist Ralph Cudworth (whose work is known to have been an influence on Locke's argument), the forms of things, and the secondary qualities they exhibit (such as colors), can be accommodated within a corpuscularian framework only if they are reinterpreted as projections of the mind. Intrinsically, the material world is just a vast system of colorless, odorless, tasteless, soundless particles; it is our minds that classify certain clusters of these particles into kinds of substances sharing a certain form, and it is our minds which perceive them, falsely, as if they really possessed features resembling our ideas of secondary qualities. A corpuscularian theorist needn't explain how physical things manifest such features, then, because they don't really have them objectively in the first place. But if this is true of the material world in general, it is no less true of that part of it we identify with our brains and bodies, which like everything else in the physical world are mere collections of colorless, odorless, tasteless, soundless particles. It follows that such mental phenomena as the ideas we have of sensory qualities – what contemporary philosophers would call "qualia," or the subjective characteristics of conscious experiences (such as the way red looks, the way a piece of music sounds, or the way pain feels) – cannot possibly be identified with any physical properties of the brain or nervous system.

Here Cudworth anticipated a line of argument developed in recent years by Thomas Nagel. The way reductionistic scientific explanation works, Nagel argues, is by carving off the subjective element of any phenomenon it seeks to explain and relegating it to the mind. Heat and cold, for example, get redefined in terms of molecular motion, with the subjective feel of heat and cold reinterpreted as entirely mind-dependent; colors get redefined in terms of various degrees of surface reflectancy of physical objects, with the subjective appearance of colors also pushed into the mind; and so forth. When it comes to the attempt to provide a reductive explanation of the mind itself, though, this strategy is closed off. The subjective element of the phenomenon to be explained cannot in this case be dealt with by relocating it into the mind, because here the subjective element just *is* the phenomenon to be explained, and there is nowhere left to relocate it. So a reductionist scientific explanation of the mind seems in principle impossible. If matter is just whatever you get when you strip away the subjective appearances through which we perceive it, those subjective appearances themselves cannot be material. And this follows, again, from the corpuscularian conception of matter that Cudworth, Locke, and so many other early modern philosophers and scientists were committed to – a conception to which the notion of matter held by contemporary materialists is, as Nagel has stressed, relevantly similar.

Some commentators have nevertheless objected that Locke's acknowledgment that matter that is "fitly disposed" can have mental properties superadded to it seems implicitly to give away the game to materialism. For if a material system's being organized in the right way makes it, even in Locke's view, a more suitable candidate for the superaddition of mental properties, how can we rule out the possibility that the right sort of organization might generate such properties all by itself, without the need for divine intervention? But this objection fails to distinguish between a *necessary* and a *sufficient* condition for the having of mental properties. Consider, by way of analogy, the relationship between a written sentence and the set of physical shapes or marks that instantiates it. There is nothing intrinsic to the physical properties of the set of squiggles that you make in writing out the sentence "The cat is on the mat" that gives it the meaning that the cat is on the mat, or that makes it a sentence at all. In itself it is just a set of ink markings, and nothing more; it counts as a sentence only because we have certain linguistic conventions according to which certain sets of shapes count as letters, words, sentences and the like. This remains true even though the structure of ink, and of the paper we write on with it, makes them "fitly disposed" for the writing out of sentences – more fitly disposed than, say, cigarette smoke, or mercury, or droplets of water, which are too formless and ephemeral to be of much use in writing sentences. Some material structures are more suitable for instantiating sentences than others are, but it does not follow that any material structure can by itself, in virtue of nothing more than its material properties, count as a sentence. Having a certain material structure, that is to say, is a necessary, but not a sufficient, condition for counting as a sentence. And Locke's point about matter which is fitly disposed to have mental properties superadded to it by God is a similar one: some material structures (e.g. brains) might be better suited to the instantiation of mental properties than others (e.g. single atoms), but it does not follow that any material structure could of itself ever count as a mind.

The dualistic component of Locke's argument certainly seems, then, to be at the very least defensible. But what of the other components? Here matters are trickier. A standard criticism of the first stage of the argument is that it seems to commit a rather blatant fallacy, in that from the claim that there must always have been something in existence, it does not follow that there is some one thing that has always existed – it could be that there has instead always been *something or other* in existence, one thing preceded by another, which was preceded by another, and so on *ad infinitum* for all of past time, but without any individual one of them having always existed. Now this objection is not by itself as telling as is often supposed. Locke could reply that if we think of the series in question as a series of material things, it is highly unlikely that such a series could have kept going for an infinite number of years; eventually, through sheer chance, there would surely have come a point already at which all material things then in existence went out of existence together. If the only things that exist or ever did exist are such material objects, then, the world would not exist now, for there would, after the point in past time just described, have been nothing left to bring the world back into being once every material thing died out. So there must in fact be an eternal being which has kept the world in existence continuously.

A rejoinder to such a reply, though, would be to say that this "eternal being" might, for all that has been said, be nothing more than the collection of basic material elements out of which all individual material things are composed. Even if every particular material object comes into and goes out of existence at some point, the set of fundamental corpuscles (or some suitable candidate from modern physics) *as a whole* remains in existence throughout. Of course, Locke would say that this collection of material elements could never by itself generate perception, knowledge, and other mental properties, and I have suggested that he has good reason for saying this. But that is consistent with the claim that, wherever the material world got the mental properties that are conjoined with (parts of) it, it has nevertheless existed eternally. This would be consistent with the idea of a "demiurge," a god who merely orders preexisting materials into a cosmos, but it would not be consistent with the traditional monotheistic conception of God as a creator who brings the world into existence out of nothing – a conception that is not only the one that Locke happens to want to defend in the *Essay*, but which is, as we shall see in the next chapter, absolutely crucial to the political philosophy he wants to defend in the *Second Treatise of Government*.

For Locke to get to the God of traditional monotheism, then, he will have to argue that even an infinitely old collection of basic material components must itself be explained in terms of God's creative action. And to do this would seem to require appealing to the idea that matter, being contingent, can only be explained by reference to something that exists necessarily or non-contingently. But this would in turn require the endorsement of some explanatory principle that could license the inference in question – a principle like the *per se* causal series of the Scholastics, or the Principle of Sufficient Reason associated with Leibniz and other rationalist philosophers. As an empiricist, though, Locke would seem to be in no position to advance such a principle. As noted earlier, Hume and other later empiricists have argued compellingly that if we take seriously the thesis that we can have no idea that is not derived from experience, it seems that we can have no idea of a "necessary connection" between causes and effects, and thus no grounds for any inference to the effect that the material world simply must have its source in some immaterial necessary being, *à la* Scholasticism and rationalism. Something similar could be said of the principle Locke appeals to in defense of the claim that the cause of a thing must be the source of its powers – a principle that Locke borrows from his Scholastic predecessors, but which does not sit well with his empiricist scruples.

If something like Locke's argument for God's existence can be defended, then (and there are several contemporary philosophers who would defend an argument for an eternal First Cause of the world), it seems that it will have to be done on the basis of a general metaphysical picture other than the sort allowed for by his empiricism. Once again, we see that Locke's attempt to preserve some elements of the Scholastic inheritance while jettisoning others may threaten to force him into a dilemma: in this case, he can either give up a thoroughgoing empiricism and salvage his argument for God's existence, or follow out the implications of his empiricism and give up the argument. It is not clear that he can have both the empiricism and the argument, though. (Whether some other argument for God's existence can be defended on empiricist but non-Lockean lines – Berkeley's argument, for example – is another question.)

Knowledge

The last book of Locke's *Essay* deals not only with our knowledge of the existence of God, but with knowledge in general, which Locke defines as "nothing but *the perception of the connexion and agreement, or disagreement and repugnancy of any of our ideas*. In this alone it consists" (E 4.1.2). Where we do not have a perception of either some essential connection between ideas or an essential incompatibility between them, we do not, strictly speaking, *know*, but merely "fancy, guess, or believe" (ibid.). Such agreement or disagreement between ideas can manifest itself in four different ways: first, in judgments of "*identity*, or *diversity*," as when we perceive that white is white and that white is not red (E 4.1.4); second, in grasping "*the relation between any two ideas*," as when we grasp that the angles of a triangle must add up to 180 degrees, where there is a necessary logical connection between the ideas in question (E 4.1.5); third, in perceiving the "*co-existence*, or *non-co-existence* in the same subject*" of two properties, where the connection is in this case not a necessary or logical one, as in our perception that yellowness and malleability are always instantiated together in gold (E 4.1.6); and fourth, in our knowledge of the "*actual real existence* agreeing to any idea," as when we judge that there really is a substance in the world corresponding to our idea of gold (E 4.1.7).

Now in some of these cases our knowledge is *a priori*. Accordingly, though on Locke's brand of empiricism, all our *concepts* derive from experience, he does not hold that all our *knowledge* does. In this respect, at least, his views overlap with those of Descartes, and they overlap also in Locke's insistence that strict knowledge entails certainty. But Locke also holds that our knowledge comes in degrees. What is most evident is what we have "*intuitive knowledge*" of, where the mind perceives a direct connection or inconsistency between ideas, such as "that *three* are more than *two*, and equal to *one* and *two*" or "that a *circle* is not a *triangle*" (E 4.2.1). The next most evident sort of knowledge is "demonstrative" in nature, and involves the grasping of an indirect connection or incompatibility between two ideas via a proof that sets out the intervening ideas that link them (E 4.2.2–3). This is the sort of knowledge we gain when carrying out a mathematical or logical derivation. The third and lowest degree of knowledge is "sensitive" knowledge of particular things immediately presented to our senses, such as the awareness you have of this book as you see and touch it here and now, which, though it is in Locke's view less evident than either our intuitive or demonstrative grasp of the connections between ideas, still counts as knowledge (E 4.2.14). So certainty is not an all-or-nothing matter. Still, anything falling short of the degree of certainty afforded by intuition, demonstration, or sensation, even if it has a very high degree of probability, cannot in Locke's view count as knowledge, but falls under the category of "opinion."

What, then, can we have genuine knowledge of? Not nearly as much as we might at first have supposed. For instance, in Locke's view we probably cannot have knowledge of the real essences of physical substances; and therefore, since the sciences are supposed to provide us with knowledge, it is likely that at least in the strictest sense "natural philosophy" – the study of the physical substances making up the natural world, what we would today call physics, chemistry, and the like – "is not capable of being made a science" (E 4.12.10). This is a surprising conclusion coming from someone who wants to serve as an "under-labourer" for the likes of Newton and Boyle. But it follows from Locke's conception of knowledge, and not merely because of his view that knowledge requires certainty. Recall that for Locke, the real essence of a physical substance is that on which its nominal essence depends; the real essence of gold, for example, is whatever inner constitution (presumably corpuscular, in Locke's view) determines that gold manifests such properties as yellowness, malleability, and so forth. And this dependence is a matter of logical necessity: that a substance has the specific properties constituting its nominal essence follows deductively, in Locke's view, from its having the real essence it does, just as a theorem of geometry follows from basic axioms and definitions (E 4.6.11). To know the real essence of a physical substance, then, we would have to know what specific aspects of its inner constitution logically necessitate that it has the properties it has by virtue of its nominal essence. But it is unlikely that we can ever discover inner properties that bear such a strong relationship to the observable properties of a physical substance. This is especially unlikely when we consider that we cannot discover any essential connection between the primary qualities of physical objects and the sensations they tend to produce in us by virtue of their secondary qualities (E 4.3.13). For example, we cannot discover any necessary connection between gold's having a certain corpuscular structure (or whatever the relevant physical facts are) and its tending to produce in us what contemporary philosophers would call yellowish qualia, where gold's appearing yellowish to us is part of its nominal essence. For reasons hinted at in the previous section, and which are familiar to contemporary philosophers of mind, it is at the very least extremely difficult to see how any configuration of purely material properties could logically necessitate the presence of yellowish sensations, or of any other sensations for that matter. Since such properties are all that physics and related disciplines have any realistic hope of giving us, though, and since they fail fully to explain the nominal essences of physical substances, it seems that these disciplines cannot give us genuine knowledge of real essences.

It is important not to overstate Locke's pessimism. He does not deny that "natural philosophy" can be useful, and that its claims are often highly probable; he denies only that such claims deserve the label "knowledge," as opposed to justified belief. Even so, Locke's view might seem implausible considering the enormous advances physics, chemistry, and the other physical sciences have made since his time. It might also seem to conflict with his confidence that the real essences of physical substances are ultimately corpuscular in nature; for if no arrangement of corpuscles would seem to necessitate the having of a substance's observable properties, why assume that its corpuscular structure has anything to do with its real essence? It seems plausible, though, that both of these objections might be answered on Locke's behalf by appealing to a *structuralist* conception of matter. The most prominent defender of this view in the twentieth century was Bertrand Russell, who developed it in the course of defending a broadly Lockean conception of our knowledge of the physical world. On a structuralist view, what physics describes for us is an abstract network, with each node in the network defined in terms of the causal role it plays relative to the other elements of the network. It does not tell us what "fleshes out" the network, though – that is, what specifically are the entities that play the causal roles in question.

Physics gives us knowledge of the causal structure of the physical world, then, but not of what it is that has that structure; it tells us what the basic components of physical reality do, but not what they are. This is an interpretation of physics that dovetails with a Lockean account of perception, insofar as such an account seems to strip away from physical objects everything but those features that are specifiable in causal terms, relegating the others to mind-dependent status; in any event, structuralism and a broadly Lockean view of perception went hand in hand in Russell's own philosophy. And if structuralism is true, then there is a clear sense in which even modern physics, with all its theoretical power and technological applicability, does not reveal to us the real essences of things, since it does not tell us even what the basic components of reality are that generate the observable properties of physical substances, let alone how those components necessitate such observable properties. But there is also a sense in which it would nevertheless be reasonable, on the structuralist view, for Locke to hold that corpuscularianism tells us *something* about the real essences of material things – namely that, whatever the ultimate constituents of reality happen to be, they play causal roles of the sort specified by corpuscularian theory.

If what we today think of as the core disciplines of empirical science cannot in Locke's view generate true knowledge, but at most highly probable opinion, things are different with the more mundane awareness we have of the physical objects of our everyday perceptual experience. Here, as we have seen, Locke thinks we have what he calls "sensitive" knowledge. But his account is notoriously problematic, since given skeptical arguments of the sort Descartes famously examined, it seems possible that our perceptions might be entirely delusory; and Locke's attempts to defend the reliability of sense perception in the face of such arguments seem question-begging and, by his own admission, fall short of demonstration (E 4.11). Of course, Locke might argue, as many contemporary philosophers would, that belief in the existence of the external physical world can be defended as a kind of quasi-scientific hypothesis that better explains the evidence of our experience than do the strange hypotheses put forward in skeptical arguments. But if this sort of method can provide us with mere probable opinion at best in the case of physics and chemistry, rather than knowledge (since in Locke's view knowledge entails certainty), it is hard to see how it could be appealed to in defense of Locke's claim that sensation provides us with genuine knowledge.

Less problematic, on Locke's conception of knowledge, is mathematics. Here genuine knowledge clearly is possible on a Lockean view, because the subject matter of mathematics concerns modes (e.g. such geometrical modes as triangularity), and as we saw earlier, there is in the case of modes no gap between their nominal essences and their real essences. The requirement that knowledge of a thing's real essence requires knowledge of the properties that necessitate the properties comprising its nominal essence is thus in this case automatically fulfilled. Perhaps more surprisingly for contemporary readers, Locke also thinks that knowledge, and thus certainty, is possible in morality, since morality too is concerned with modes (e.g. goodness). And as the previous section indicated, he believes as well that we can know, via demonstration, that God exists. He is sketchy, at least in the *Essay*, about how knowledge of interesting specific moral truths might be arrived at. But as we will see in the next chapter, he does attempt in the *Second Treatise of Government* to justify some substantial moral claims, and knowledge of God's existence will be a key presupposition of his argument. As we noted at the beginning of this chapter, a concern to vindicate the possibility of moral and religious knowledge was, in any event, the initial impetus for embarking on the project of writing the *Essay*. In Locke's estimation, whatever limitations there might be on our knowledge of the physical world, human beings yet "have light enough to lead them to the knowledge of their maker, and the sight of their own duties," and with this they "have reason to be well satisfied" (E 1.1.5).

This naturally brings us to a final component of Locke's theory of knowledge, namely his account of the relationship between faith and reason. As we have noted before, Locke is always concerned to defend individual liberty of thought against the claims of rationalists and ecclesiastical authorities (especially, in his mind, Catholic ones), who would, as he sees it, shackle our minds with bogus "innate" ideas and unfounded dogmas, respectively. This concern is at the forefront of his account of faith. But no less important to him is the need to prevent epistemological liberty from degenerating into license and irrationality. Another target of his account is therefore the "enthusiasm" of some of the Puritan sects of his day, whose adherents tended to justify their commitment to their idiosyncratic beliefs via an appeal to private revelation and subjective religious experience.

Locke's answer to all such opponents begins with the affirmation that "*reason* must be our last judge and guide in everything" (E 4.19.14). In saying this, he does not mean to deny the proper place of either revelation or faith. "Whatever God hath revealed, is certainly true; no doubt can be made of it," Locke affirms; and this, he goes on to say "is the proper object of *faith*" (E 4.18.10). For faith, in his view, is just "the assent to any proposition ... as coming from God, in some extraordinary way of communication" (E 4.18.2). Obviously, if there is a God who is all-knowing and all-good, whatever he reveals must be true, so that to have faith in what he says can hardly be irrational. But of course, that just raises the question of when we can be justified in believing that God really has revealed something to us. On this question, Locke says, "*reason* must judge" (E 4.18.10). Accordingly, faith must always rest upon reason. We can never be justified in claiming something to be true on the basis of revelation unless we can establish by reason alone that the revelation in question really took place.

This sort of view is certainly a challenge to the "enthusiasts" Locke was so concerned to refute. It is difficult to see how an appeal to nothing more than a personal religious experience can, all by itself, serve as conclusive grounds for claiming that God has revealed some truth; certainly no one could reasonably expect many other people to believe that such a revelation occurred to him based on nothing more than his own say so. But it is not clear why Locke's account of the relationship between faith and reason should be regarded as a challenge to the medieval Catholic view that was Locke's other target. The medieval Church did not rest its doctrinal claims on any private revelation; indeed, it consistently held (in opposition to Gnosticism, for example) that no authoritative teaching of the Church could be based on anything other than publicly accessible sources, such as the deliverances of tradition. Nor was the appeal to tradition itself nothing more than a roundabout appeal to "faith," if that is meant to imply an arbitrary commitment of the will to believe something without evidence, or even contrary to the evidence. That sort of understanding of faith, however common today, would have been foreign to a medieval thinker like Aquinas. For Aquinas, the "preamble" to faith was the demonstration, through purely philosophical arguments, of the existence of God and the immortality of the soul, and also the defense on purely rational grounds of such distinctively Christian claims as that Jesus Christ was resurrected from the dead, that the claims he made about himself before the crucifixion were thereby vindicated, and that he established, through his Apostles, an ongoing institutional Church whose function it is to preserve and provide an authoritative interpretation of his teachings, where these teachings are precisely what the content of the tradition consists of. To have faith is just to assent to these teachings; and though they are believed to be Christ's own teachings on the basis of the authority of the Church, the trustworthiness of that authority is something that can, on the medieval Christian view, itself be defended through reason. Faith, then, is not in conflict with reason; indeed, it presupposes reason.

Now of course, Locke would no doubt deny that there is such an authoritative Church or tradition. But this would seem to be a difference over details rather than over principle. The basic idea that faith in a proposition allegedly revealed by God must be based on a rational defense of the claim that the proposition was in fact so revealed is one that seems to have been accepted by the medievals no less than by Locke. Moreover, whatever one thinks of the Catholic conception of an authoritative tradition, it does at least attempt to provide some systematic criterion for sifting genuinely revealed propositions from bogus ones: those claims that have been a part of the tradition since the time of Christ's

Apostles, or which are entailed by such claims, are on the Catholic view to be considered authoritative revelations; those that have no such standing are not authoritative. By contrast, Locke, though he recommends believing only what can be shown by reason genuinely to have been revealed, says little or nothing about how one might go about determining this. (To appeal to the Bible, as he sometimes does, does not solve the problem, since that just raises the question of why one ought to believe that the Bible is a genuine source of divine revelation. The medieval Catholic view would be that the Bible is authoritative precisely because it is a part of the overall tradition that the Church has preserved from the time of Christ; but it is not clear what Locke would put in the place of this defense of biblical authority. He certainly could not, consistently with his attack on "enthusiasm," endorse the suggestion made by some Protestants that the authority of the Bible is evident from a divinely granted subjective sense of assurance.)

In addition to the theological questions raised by Locke's position, there are purely philosophical ones too. Locke's hostility to the medieval view of tradition and authority went hand in hand with his commitment to a kind of epistemological individualism, the idea (another one he shares with Descartes) that a rationally justified belief is one that the individual arrives at entirely on the basis of his own epistemic resources. In Locke's view, we must be free to think things through, from scratch, for ourselves; authority and tradition can only be obstacles to this. Obviously, this is a view bound to seem self-evident to most contemporary readers. But it can be challenged. On the view of conservative thinkers like Edmund Burke (1729–97) and F. A. Hayek (1899–1992), the individual human mind is too limited to be capable of working out the complicated truth about human affairs all on its own. There are too many variables to consider, and too little evidence available to any single person or even any single generation. But tradition provides us with a shortcut to finding out what we need to know. For moral beliefs and social institutions that do not reflect the deepest aspects of human nature are unlikely to survive for very long, or, if they do survive, they are unlikely to predominate among a very large population. By contrast, those beliefs and institutions that have tended to survive for a very long time and across various cultures are likely to reflect something deep in human nature, otherwise they would probably not have survived. Since tradition is the repository of such long-lasting beliefs and institutions, then, it deserves our respect. It might not be infallible, but it ought to get the benefit of the doubt. For given that it encapsulates the results of a centuries old trial-and-error process that takes account of more information than could possibly be accessed all at once by any individual mind, it is, in a sense, "wiser" than any individual mind. To thrust tradition aside in the name of individual freedom of thought is thus the opposite of rational – it is a rash and arrogant failure to grasp one's own limitations.

A related but distinct line of thought has been pursued by the contemporary philosopher Alasdair MacIntyre, who argues that genuine intellectual progress, when it occurs at all, tends to occur only in the context of a tradition of thought whose adherents are committed to the common project of working out systematically the implications of the tradition's basic assumptions, resolving the problems that beset it, and so forth. Through the disagreements and debate that arise between defenders of alternative interpretations of the tradition, its full ramifications and ultimate coherence and defensibility, or lack thereof, are progressively laid bare, and this is a process that might take centuries to play out. A successful tradition is one that can resolve its problems and generate new directions of inquiry that build on what has come before; a failed tradition is one that is incapable of doing so, and which tends to stagnate into repetition and pedantry or even to disintegrate altogether. Either way, it is not the individual thinker spinning out a novel theory from the comfort of his armchair who is the paradigm of rationality; rather, reason always works within a social context, and against a background of presuppositions that the individual thinker inherited rather than invented.

Of course, all of this raises many questions. The point, however, is not to settle here the debate over the relative merits of tradition and authority versus individual freedom of inquiry. It is rather merely to indicate that there is indeed a real debate to be had, and that Locke's view, though almost universally (if unreflectively) endorsed by modern people, is not necessarily unchallengeable.

Conclusion

We have seen that the views Locke develops within the *Essay* have been extremely influential, but also that many of the arguments he gives in their defense are seriously problematic, and are often widely acknowledged to be so. This is surely a rather curious fact. As Gilbert Ryle once asked, "Why is it that although nearly every youthful student of philosophy both can and does in about his second essay refute Locke's entire Theory of Knowledge, yet Locke made a bigger difference to the whole intellectual climate of mankind than anyone had done since Aristotle?"

The trend among contemporary Locke scholars is, it seems, to answer that it is a mistake to view Locke's case for his overall philosophical vision – comprising an empiricist account of the origin of our ideas, the primary/secondary quality distinction, the corpuscularian theory of matter, an anti-Aristotelian view of essences and species, a memory theory of personal identity, and so on and so forth – as resting primarily on the several specific and sometimes problematic arguments he presents in defense of each of these components individually. Rather, what Locke is doing is suggesting that his philosophy, considered as a systematic whole, is on balance a more plausible way of accounting for the evidence of our ordinary experience and the findings of modern science than is the Scholastic worldview he seeks to replace. It is the big picture rather than the details that concern him, and the probability rather than certainty of his position that he seeks to establish. And judged by this standard, those who put forward this interpretation might say, Locke was successful enough that it should be no surprise that his philosophy has been as influential as it has been.

But such an answer does not seem wholly satisfactory. For one thing, as we have seen, some of Locke's objections to Scholastic views seem to rest on misunderstandings or uncharitable readings of those views. If Locke can show that his views are more plausible than the ones he criticizes, then, this can hardly serve to establish the superiority of his philosophy over Scholasticism if the views he criticizes are not in fact genuinely Scholastic ones in the first place. Secondly, Locke's positions arguably often create as many problems as they solve. His property dualism, for example, has in common with all post-Cartesian forms of dualism that it makes the causal relationship between mind and matter utterly mysterious; indeed, Locke himself held that we would likely never be able to understand exactly how physical processes give rise to the sensory qualities or qualia that characterize our conscious experiences. Of course, many contemporary philosophers would opt instead for a materialist conception of the mind, but all extant materialist theories have notorious problems of their own. The Scholastics had the notion of formal causation to help elucidate the relationship between the soul, understood as the substantial form of the body, and the material world; Locke and other moderns, rejecting as they do the notions of form and formal causation, arguably both created a gulf between mind and matter and deprived themselves of any way to bridge it. And then there is the way in which Lockean views often seem to have implications that are highly counter-intuitive and, at the very least, open to dispute. We have seen, for instance, that a Lockean approach to personal identity seems entirely to separate being a human being from being a person, and, when taken in the direction contemporary writers like Parfit have gone with it, may even entail the abandonment of the concept of a person altogether. Locke's empiricist theory of concept acquisition is notoriously difficult to square with the ideas of substance and objective causal connection. His account of language seems excessively subjectivist, making it mysterious how inter-subjective communication is possible, and his views on the nature of classification and species are radically, and controversially, anti-realist. His account of free will is similarly controversial. And so on. None of this proves that the Lockean views in question are wrong, of course; but it does suggest that it is by no means obvious that Locke's philosophy is less problematic than Scholasticism.

Thirdly, it is not at all clear that an empiricist like Locke could sincerely claim merely to be offering a better explanation of the data both he and his rivals share in common; for an empiricist view of the origins of our ideas puts rather stringent constraints on what the empiricist is prepared to count as data in the first place. So, for example, if a Scholastic (or rationalist) philosopher were to object that empiricism cannot do justice to our ideas of objective causal connections or physical substances, an empiricist may well reply (*à la* Hume or Berkeley): "So much for objective causal connections and physical substances, then; we must not really have any such ideas at all." Such a view might be defensible, but it can hardly be said to rest on a neutral conception of what the evidence is that a good philosophical theory ought to be able to account for. In general, a complaint that Scholastic and rationalist thinkers might reasonably make against Locke and other empiricists is that from their point of view, the right order of inquiry is first to establish what concepts we actually have and then come up with a theory to try to explain how we got them; empiricism, by contrast, first comes up with a theory about where our concepts come from and then deduces from it what concepts we actually have. This procedure is open to the charge that it has things methodologically backwards, and "stacks the deck" in favor of empiricism, defining out of existence any possible counterevidence. Certainly it ought to make us pause before too glibly accepting the claim that Locke's philosophy constitutes a better explanation of the evidence. What counts as "the evidence" is precisely what is in dispute between Locke and his opponents.

A more plausible answer to the question posed by Ryle is, I think, the one Ryle himself proposed. The attraction of Locke's philosophy, he suggested, was that its rather deflationary account of knowledge seemed to make possible a way of defusing the fierce, indeed sometimes violent, political and religious disputes that characterized the times in which he wrote. If there is in fact very little that we can be said, strictly speaking, to know – and if, in particular, apart from God's existence and the other metaphysical preconditions of morality, there is very little in the way of metaphysical truth that we can ever hope to discover – then the religious and political disputes that rest on disagreements over metaphysical questions would seem to have no reasonable foundation. Parties to these disputes ought to lay down their arms and agree to disagree, confining to the private sphere their controversial beliefs and keeping them out of the public square. Toleration would seem to be the only rational policy where real knowledge is impossible.

If this interpretation is correct, then the ultimate import of the seemingly abstruse metaphysical and epistemological doctrines developed in Locke's *Essay* is practical and political. Of course, the fact that a philosophical position might have certain practical and political advantages does not entail that it is true. The question of whether Locke's metaphysical and epistemological doctrines are in the end defensible thus cannot be avoided. But if his ultimate point in trying to defend them is to provide a foundation for a certain kind of political philosophy, a consideration of that political philosophy is in order if we are going to understand exactly what sort of metaphysical and epistemological views Locke really needs for political purposes to commit himself to, and which, if any, he might be able to jettison. This brings us at last to Locke's two most famous works in political philosophy, which will be the subject of the next two chapters.

FURTHER READING

R. S. Woolhouse's *Locke* (Minneapolis: University of Minnesota Press, 1983) and Michael Ayers' two-volume study *Locke* (London: Routledge, 1991) are two important studies of the *Essay*. Most of the works cited at the end of chapter 1 also discuss the *Essay* in detail. Other important studies include: Jonathan Bennett, *Locke, Berkeley, Hume: Central Themes* (Oxford: Clarendon Press, 1971), E. J. Lowe, *Locke on Human Understanding* (London: Routledge, 1995), J. L. Mackie, *Problems from Locke* (Oxford: Clarendon Press, 1976), and J. W. Yolton, *Locke and the Compass of Human Understanding* (Cambridge: Cambridge University Press, 1970). Vere Chappell, ed., *Locke* (Oxford: Oxford University Press, 1998) and Ian C. Tipton, ed., *Locke on Human Understanding* (Oxford: Oxford University Press, 1977) are collections of essays on various topics in the *Essay*. Gary Fuller, Robert Stecker, and John P. Wright, eds., *John Locke: An Essay Concerning Human Understanding in Focus* (London: Routledge, 2000) contains selections from the *Essay* together with critical essays by several prominent Locke scholars.

Studies of various particular themes from the *Essay* include Peter Alexander, *Ideas, Qualities, and Corpuscles: Locke and Boyle on the External World* (Cambridge: Cambridge University Press, 1985), Walter R. Ott, *Locke's Philosophy of Language* (Cambridge: Cambridge University Press, 2004), Nicholas Wolterstorff, *John Locke and the Ethics of Belief* (Cambridge: Cambridge University Press, 1996), R. S. Woolhouse, *Locke's Philosophy of Science and Knowledge* (Oxford: Blackwell, 1971), Gideon Yaffe, *Liberty Worth the Name: Locke on Free Agency* (Princeton, NJ: Princeton University Press, 2000), J. W. Yolton, *John Locke and the Way of Ideas* (Oxford: Clarendon Press, 1956), and John W. Yolton, *The Two Intellectual Worlds of John Locke. Man, Person, and Spirits in the "Essay"* (Ithaca: Cornell University Press, 2004).

G. W. Leibniz's *New Essays on Human Understanding* is a classic contemporary critique of Locke's *Essay*, and is available in a new edition edited by Peter Remnant and Jonathan Bennett (Cambridge: Cambridge University Press, 1996). Berkeley's *Principles of Human Knowledge* and *Three Dialogues Between Hylas and Philonous* are available in several editions, as are Hume's *Treatise of Human Nature* and *Enquiry Concerning Human Understanding* and Reid's *Essays on the Intellectual Powers of Man*. Cudworth's works are less readily available, but Ayers' *Locke* provides a useful summary of the aspects of Cudworth's thought most relevant to the study of Locke.

James Tyrell's remark about the conversation that led Locke to write the *Essay* is cited by Woolhouse in the Introduction to his edition of the *Essay*. Peter Geach's critique of abstractionism is to be found in his book *Mental Acts* (London: Routledge and Kegan Paul, 1958). John Haldane discusses the "Prime Thinker" in a book co-written with J. J. C. Smart, *Atheism and Theism*, 2nd edition (Oxford: Blackwell, 2003). This book also comprises an excellent introduction to the current state of the debate over the traditional arguments for God's existence. Gottlob Frege's essay "Thought" is available in Michael Beaney, ed., *The Frege Reader* (Oxford: Blackwell, 1997). Excerpts from Hume and Reid most relevant to Locke's theory of personal identity are reprinted in John Perry, ed., *Personal Identity* (Berkeley: University of California Pres, 1975), as is Butler's essay "Of Personal Identity." Derek Parfit's views on personal identity are also represented in the Perry anthology, and developed at length in his *Reasons and Persons* (Oxford: Clarendon Press, 1984). Edward Feser, *Philosophy of Mind: A Short Introduction* (Oxford: Oneworld, 2005) provides an overview of the current debate concerning the mind-body problem. Thomas Nagel's influential article "What is it Like to Be a Bat?"

is available in his book *Mortal Questions* (Cambridge: Cambridge University Press, 1979). Bertrand Russell's structuralism is developed at length in his *The Analysis of Matter* (London: Kegan Paul, 1927) and lucidly summarized in his *My Philosophical Development* (London: Unwin Paperbacks, 1985). Burke's views are developed in his classic *Reflections on the Revolution in France*, available in several editions. F. A. Hayek's views are developed in *The Fatal Conceit* (Chicago: University of Chicago Press, 1989) and examined in Edward Feser, "Hayek on Tradition," *Journal of Libertarian Studies*, Vol. 17, No. 1 (Winter 2003). Alasdair MacIntyre's views are expounded in *After Virtue*, 2nd edition (Notre Dame: University of Notre Dame Press, 1984).

Gilbert Ryle's remark is from his essay "John Locke," reprinted in Jean S. Yolton, ed., *A Locke Miscellany* (Bristol: Thoemmes, 1990).

Chapter Four

The Second Treatise of Government

The Two Treatises in context

> We hold these Truths to be self-evident, that all Men are
> created equal, that they are endowed by their Creator with
> certain unalienable Rights, that among these are Life, Lib-
> erty, and the Pursuit of Happiness – That to secure these
> Rights, Governments are instituted among Men, deriving
> their just powers from the Consent of the Governed, that
> whenever any Form of Government becomes destructive
> of these Ends, it is the Right of the People to alter or to
> abolish it, and to institute new Government.

Thus wrote Thomas Jefferson in the American *Declaration of Independence,* and it is well known that his words
were inspired by Locke's political philosophy. Though
there were certainly other intellectual influences on Jefferson and the other American founding fathers (such as the
classical republicanism rooted in the Greek and Roman
traditions of political thought), there can be little doubt
that in the founding principles of the United States we see
as pure and direct an implementation of Lockean theory
as has ever existed.

To be sure, Jefferson's formulation is by no means
entirely Lockean in content. Locke would, for reasons we

LOCKE

will examine presently, be more inclined to speak of rights to one's "life, health, liberty [and] possessions" (T II.6), though the pursuit of happiness is not entirely outside the range of his concern. More significantly, he would deny that our rights are "unalienable" and that their existence is "self-evident," if this latter claim is meant to imply that our knowledge of the existence of rights is "intuitive" in the sense described in the previous chapter. He would reject the latter claim as inconsistent with his epistemological thesis that only the grasp of a direct conceptual connection between ideas provides a degree of certainty indicative of self-evidence or intuitive knowledge, for it is implausible that "Human beings have rights" has the analytic character that "All triangles are three-sided" has. He would reject the claim that all our rights are "unalienable" on the grounds that rights violators forfeit their own rights by virtue of their wrongdoing, that property rights are of their very nature alienable insofar as a property owner has the right to sell or give away what he or she owns, and that all individuals renounce their right to punish rights violators by leaving the state of nature and entering into political society.

That human beings have the rights they do only insofar as these rights are "endowed by their Creator" is, however, a very Lockean thesis indeed. To be sure, Locke is, as is commonly recognized, a "natural rights" theorist; that is to say, he takes our rights to be in some sense natural to us, built into the human condition rather than being merely an artifact of convention or consensus. This is central to his political philosophy, for the strict limits he wants to put on the power of government over the individual can exist only if there is something in the very nature of things that requires that those limits be there, something that human beings cannot take it upon themselves to change. But Locke also holds that that something is nothing less than the will of God.

Now some have denied that this traditional understanding of Locke's position is correct. Leo Strauss, for example, famously held that Locke was no more a sincere believer in God than Hobbes was, and that his reference to a divine source of rights is a mere smokescreen intended to veil from the *hoi polloi* his true, quasi-Hobbesian agenda. But while this thesis still has defenders today, it has been rejected by most Locke scholars, and for good reason. As we saw in the previous chapter, Locke's argument for God's existence is one he devotes a fair amount of space and effort to developing. He does not seem to be merely "going through the motions" for the sake of avoiding controversy, and given that some of the other positions he took *were* theologically controversial, maintaining an insincere appearance of orthodoxy does not appear to have been an overriding concern for him. Furthermore, the specific kind of argument he gives was one that other, clearly sincere, believers such as Cudworth also endorsed, so there is nothing about its content that should make us suspicious. Indeed, in emphasizing as he does the idea that mental properties are inexplicable in material terms, and that only an immaterial deity could possibly explain the origin of such properties in a material universe, Locke is taking a position directly at odds with Hobbes, who held that mind was fully reducible to matter and that God is Himself a kind of material being (which is one reason Hobbes has often been regarded as an atheist in disguise, since immateriality has traditionally been taken to be an essential property of God). This would seem an odd argument for a closet Hobbesian even to pretend to endorse. In any event, as we will see, Locke's theory of rights in fact absolutely *requires* a theological foundation. Given his broader metaphysical commitments, if he cannot appeal to God as a source of natural rights, there is nothing else he can appeal to.

All the same, Locke was firmly opposed to the way certain other religious believers had appealed to God in defense of their favored political doctrines. Chief among the views to which he objected were those of Sir Robert Filmer (1588–1653), who in his book *Patriarcha; or, The Natural Power of Kings* (1680) argued that kings rule by divine right. Filmer held that royal authority was a kind of paternal authority, and has been inherited by existing kings from Adam, who by virtue of being the father of the human race was also the first king. This view was the target of Locke's *First Treatise of Government*, wherein he argues that (1) Adam did not in fact have royal authority over his children, either by virtue of fatherhood or by divine mandate, (2) even if he had possessed such authority, none of his heirs had a right to inherit it, (3) even if any of them had such a right, there is nothing either in the natural law or God's revealed law that tells us specifically which of his heirs had it, and (4) even if we did know which of his heirs had it, there is no way at the present time to determine specifically who among those now living has inherited this right from these earlier heirs. This, at any rate, is how Locke sums up the argument of the *First Treatise* at the beginning of the *Second Treatise*, and most contemporary readers find Locke's case so decisive, and Filmer's so archaic, that few bother to look at the *First Treatise* itself any more. It is the *Second Treatise*, which is also in part directed at Filmer but which contains Locke's own positive political philosophy, which has had the greatest influence and is still widely studied. Accordingly, that is the work we will focus on in the present chapter, though we will have occasion here and there to cite themes from the *First Treatise* as well.

In Locke's attack on Filmer, we see another respect in which his views do indeed foreshadow those expressed in the *Declaration of Independence*. For Locke wants to insist against Filmer that all human beings are "created equal" in the sense that none of them has any sort of natural political authority over another. Filmer defended belief in such natural political authority by assimilating it to paternal authority. Aristotle famously (and in a way that Filmer himself rejected) defended it by appealing to the idea that those with wisdom are naturally suited to rule over those without it. While Locke did not deny that fathers have authority over their children or that some human beings are wiser than others, his view is that the content of our natural rights is such that none of these considerations can be taken to show that anyone has any natural authority over others in the political sphere. Our rights also put limits on the extent of the authority we can invest even in a government we voluntarily consent to be ruled by. Hence Locke's theory of rights is intended as a refutation not only of Filmer's doctrine of the absolute authority of kings, but also of Hobbes's social contract version of absolutism. Our equality in the political sphere is so total that we could never completely give it up even if we wanted to. (This by no means entails for Locke that we are or ought to be equal in other ways, however; indeed, as we will see, Locke's doctrine of natural rights famously tends to support a rather high degree of economic inequality.)

To be sure, there is debate among scholars over whether the *Second Treatise* was actually intended by Locke primarily as a response to Filmer or primarily as a response to Hobbes. But whatever details of interpretation might hinge on this dispute, it is enough for our purposes to understand that he clearly disagreed with and sought to undermine the views of both of these thinkers. It is also important to note, though, that his immediate aim in writing the *Second Treatise* was as practical as it was theoretical. As we saw in chapter 1, Locke was writing at a time of mounting opposition to the policies of King Charles II and his successor James II, and there can be no doubt that the work was meant to serve in support of this opposition, and that its eventual publication after the accession of William and Mary was intended as an *ex post facto* justification of the revolution. That Locke had such immediate political considerations in mind no doubt accounts at least partially for the philosophically problematic aspects many commentators see in the book, such as the elements in it that appear to be in tension with the doctrines of the *Essay*. Given that Locke was writing a tract for the times, he was less concerned than he might have otherwise been to produce a systematic treatise more clearly in harmony with his broader philosophical views.

Nevertheless, there is, of course, a significant continuity between the *Essay* and the *Second Treatise*; in particular, we see in the latter work – and in the *Letter Concerning Toleration*, which we will be looking at in the next chapter – a more thorough and explicit development of the consequences of the moral and religious themes that are always lurking in the background of the *Essay*. That Locke had urgent practical goals in mind in publishing the *Two Treatises* in just the manner and at just the time he did – so much so that he allowed the *First Treatise* to be published in an unfinished state – does not entail that his political views were not for the most part a natural byproduct of his general philosophical position. Moreover, whatever the extent to which the Glorious

Revolution influenced the concrete details of the work, the *Second Treatise* went on to be regarded as an expression of timeless principles that could be used to justify other revolutions in other places – as evidenced by the latter half of the passage from Jefferson quoted above.

The law of nature

What, specifically, are the natural rights Locke takes us to have? The beginnings of the answer lie in his affirmation that "every man has a property in his own person: this nobody has any right to but himself" (T II.27). This is a principle that has come to be known as the thesis of *self-ownership*, the idea that human beings are their own property, from which it follows that they have the rights over themselves usually entailed by ownership. Among the consequences of this for Locke is that "the labour of [a person's] body, and the work of his hands, we may say, are properly his," so that "whatsoever then he removes out of the state that nature hath provided, and left it in, he hath mixed his labour with, and joined to it something that is his own, and thereby makes it his property" (ibid.). Here we have the essence of Locke's famous "labor-mixing" theory of property in external resources: you own yourself, and thus your labor, and no one, at least initially, owns the natural resources external to us; but by "mixing" your labor with part of these resources in the act of being the first one to appropriate them, they become inextricably bound up with something you own, so that you thereby come to own the specific resources in question themselves. If you find a piece of unowned driftwood, say, and whittle it into a spear or statuette, you have thereby come to own the resulting object. The basic right of self-ownership thus generates a further right to own external resources, the sorts of things we usually think of as paradigms of private property.

We will return later to Locke's account of private property rights in external resources. For now we can note that property rights are central to Locke's account of rights in general; and this, as we will see, is crucial to his account of the foundation and source of those rights. Locke famously held that "the great and chief end ... of men's uniting into commonwealths, and putting themselves under government, is the preservation of their property" (T II.124). This is sometimes taken to be evidence that he was essentially an apologist for the propertied classes and his political philosophy an instance of what C. B. Macpherson has famously labeled the ideology of "possessive individualism." But by "property" in this passage Locke intends to refer not only to the rights one might claim over inanimate objects but also to rights over one's life and liberty, viz. over things valued even by many critics of the institution of private property as usually understood.

Now since Locke takes our rights to be "natural," it might reasonably be thought that he takes their basis to lie in natural law. And indeed, he held that "the state of nature has a law of nature to govern it, which obliges everyone: and reason, which is that law, teaches all mankind, who will but consult it, that being all equal and independent, no one ought to harm another in his life, health, liberty, or possessions" (T II.6). Unlike Hobbes, Locke takes our basic moral obligations to one another to exist even before any social contract has been agreed to and thus before we enter into civil society: they exist in the state of nature itself and are thus themselves "natural," both in the sense that they are not the product of human convention or agreement and in the sense that they are knowable through the natural faculty of reason.

But though Locke was clearly a natural law theorist of sorts, his conception of natural law was very different from the one associated with, say, Aquinas. As we saw in chapter 2, for Aquinas and other medieval Scholastic thinkers, the content and normative force of the natural law are essentially connected with certain metaphysical facts about human beings, such as that they partake of an objective essence that constitutes their nature, and that they have a natural end, determined by their essence, that defines the good for them. Later thinkers in the Scholastic tradition derived from a broadly Thomistic conception of natural law a doctrine of natural rights, conceived of essentially as the concomitants of the duties all human beings have toward one another to treat others in a way conducive to the realization of their natural end. As we have also seen, however, Locke rejects these metaphysical presuppositions of the Scholastic conception of natural law. He denies that we can know the real essences of things, and the nominal essences we can know are entirely the creations of the human mind and thus do not necessarily reflect any objective metaphysical reality; and his commitment to the corpuscularian and mechanistic conception of scientific explanation entails a denial of the existence of objective functions or natural ends. In short, in rejecting the epistemology and metaphysics of Scholasticism in particular and Aristotelianism in general, Locke rejected also the foundations of the medieval approach to natural law, and with it any possibility of using that approach to ground a doctrine of natural rights.

On what does he ground it, then? Like Hobbes, Locke holds that there is utility in adherence to the natural law, but unlike Hobbes he neither takes such utility to exhaust its content nor regards self-interest as the basis for our obligation to obey it. In his early *Essays on the Law of Nature*, Locke says that utility is merely "the consequence of obedience" to the natural law rather than its foundation, and explicitly denies that self-interest is its rationale (ELN 215). Also unlike Hobbes, but like the Scholastics, Locke takes there to be an ineliminable theological dimension to the law of nature. Specifically, he holds that knowledge of natural law, like knowledge of law in general in his view, must satisfy three conditions: the first two are knowledge of a lawmaker and knowledge of the lawmaker's will (ELN 151); the third is knowledge of sanctions or penalties attached to non-compliance with the law (E 2.28.6). Now the lawmaker in question in the case of the natural law is, of course, God, and it is clear why Locke held that the first condition stated here is met, given that he thought that the existence of God could be philosophically demonstrated. But what about the second and third conditions?

This question naturally brings us to Locke's most explicit statement of the foundations of natural rights, as presented in one of the most famous passages of the *Second Treatise*:

[M]en being all the workmanship of one omnipotent and infinitely wise Maker; all the servants of one sovereign Master, sent into the world by his order, and about his business; they are his property, whose workmanship they are, made to last during his, not another's pleasure. (T II.6)

In short, since God made us, God owns us, and to harm other human beings or otherwise hinder them in their realization of God's purposes for them would therefore be to violate God's property rights. This would seem to be the ground of what Locke calls "the fundamental law of nature," which is "that all, as much as may be, should be preserved" (T II.183; and see also II.16 and II.134). The basic and general imperative to preserve what belongs to God is the ground of our specific obligations not to kill, maim, and steal from one another, and thus the ground of our rights not to be harmed in these ways.

Now before we examine the bearing of this argument on the question at hand, let us pause to note its relationship to some of the other Lockean themes we have considered. To begin with, the argument might seem at first glance to contradict Locke's commitment to the thesis of self-ownership; for if we own ourselves, how could God own us? That there is no genuine contradiction here is evident, however, when we consider that it is very common to speak both of human beings owning property and of God as owning everything, and religious believers who claim to own their homes outright after having paid off their mortgages are hardly to be accused of inconsistency. Obviously what is meant in such everyday cases is that though God owns everything, he nevertheless allows us to take exclusive possession over certain parts of the world in such a way that relative to everyone else it is as if we own those things, though strictly speaking we are only "leasing" them from God. Similarly, what Locke has in mind is surely the idea that though God owns us along with everything else that exists, he nevertheless allows us to "lease" ourselves from Him in such a way that relative to each other it is as if we are self-owners. Fred and Ethel ultimately do not own themselves, for they are owned by God. But it is Fred and Fred alone who holds the lease on Fred, and Ethel and Ethel alone who holds the lease on Ethel. Consequently, Fred has no right to interfere with Ethel's use of herself, her labor, or the fruits of her labor, and Ethel has no right to interfere with Fred's use of Fred, his labor, or its fruits. By the same token, God holds Fred rather than Ethel responsible for what Fred does with what God has given him, and holds Ethel rather than Fred responsible for what he has given her.

That Locke understands self-ownership in such a fashion nevertheless has significant consequences. In particular, it is clear that his conception of self-ownership is very different from the conception held by many contemporary libertarians, including those (like Robert Nozick) who have taken their inspiration from him. Locke explicitly denies, for example, that anyone has a right to commit suicide, for killing oneself counts as a violation of God's property rights just as surely as murdering another person does (T II.6). This would seem to rule out any libertarian argument to the effect that since you own your body, you can do with it what you like, including taking drugs, engaging in illicit sex, having an abortion, or what have you. For if any of these things either harm you or are for some other reason against God's will, then it would follow that you do *not* have a right to do them (compare T I.59). For Locke, talking about self-ownership really seems to be merely shorthand for talking about the rights one has by virtue of leasing oneself from God. This might well rule out all sorts of interference in one's life by other human beings, but it does not give one carte blanche to do whatever one likes, just as your leasing an apartment might entail that others cannot enter into it without your permission, but not that you can violate the terms of your agreement with your landlord, or more generally that you can treat the apartment as if you owned it and the landlord didn't. For the same reason, there can in Locke's view be no right to sell oneself into slavery (T II.23), for such a right would entail that one can legitimately give another human being complete power over oneself, which one cannot do if one is ultimately owned by God.

It is important to note also the relationship between Locke's "workmanship of God" argument and his theory of property. As we have seen, for Locke, a property right in an external object comes into existence when one mixes one's labor, which one already owns by virtue of being a self-owner, with some unowned resource. So in the case of God's creation of the universe, including the human race, it would follow that God has "mixed his labor" with us and thereby owns us. Now as we will see, the fact that we can only mix our labor with pre-existing materials – materials we did not ourselves create and which Locke says God in some sense gave to the human race as whole – raises a number of questions about how absolute our property rights in external resources can be. In the case of God's ownership of us, no analogous questions arise. God created the universe *ex nihilo* – out of nothing, without the use of any pre-existing materials – and so there is no question of anyone having any pre-existing claim to the materials he used, for he didn't use any in the first place. His rights over what he created, including us, are accordingly absolute. This is why it was said in the previous chapter that Locke's case requires a God who created *ex nihilo* rather than a demiurge who creates out of pre-existing materials; for the latter sort of being would less clearly have the absolute property rights over us that Locke takes God to have.

It was also said earlier that Locke's appeal to God is absolutely necessary if he is to have a foundation for his conception of natural rights, and the reason should now be evident. Recall that the Scholastic worldview from which the earliest theories of natural rights developed took human beings to have an objective essence, enshrined in the substantial form that the Scholastics identified with the human soul, and that this essence entails a natural end or purpose. Rights were taken to follow from this picture of human nature as necessary preconditions of individuals being able to fulfill their natural end and live in accordance with their nature. But Locke rejects substantial forms, and with them the notions of objective essences and natural ends or purposes as the Scholastics conceived of them. Accordingly, he would seem to have no basis in human nature *per se* for a doctrine of natural rights, for on a Lockean view, human beings cannot, it seems, be the kinds of things that have the relevant sorts of natures. To be sure, Locke does sometimes appeal to nature's "intentions" and the like (T I.59); the trouble is, since he rejects Aristotelian final causes and the possibility of knowledge of real essences, it is hard to see how he can have any justification for such an appeal.

But of course, Locke also wants to deny the Hobbesian thesis that whatever rights we have are conventional rather than natural, arising only out of a social contract, and thus resting on the agreement of other human beings. If human beings are to have anything like natural rights, then, they must have them in a derivative way, getting them from someone who does have them naturally: God, who alone has any inherent rights at all, and who delegates some of them to us. And again, only a God who creates *ex nihilo* would seem to be capable of grounding such rights; for if he were merely one part of the natural order among others, using, as we do, pre-existing materials to create with, it isn't clear that he would have over us the absolute rights Locke attributes to Him. But in that case, it isn't as clear that all the ways in which we might harm each other would really be violations of God's rights after all: perhaps a Hobbesian tyrant could claim that in enslaving us, he was merely taking control over our bodies, which even God doesn't have an absolute right to since they are composed of matter he didn't Himself create.

I do not mean to imply that Locke *explicitly* reasoned in just this way; in fact his defense of natural law and natural rights in theological terms is notoriously sketchy, and does not go too far beyond the passages quoted above. My claim is rather that something like the sort of argument I have outlined in the last three paragraphs would seem to be the best way to make sense of why God plays such a large role in Locke's account of natural rights, and that a purportedly Lockean political philosophy without God (as is put forward by Nozick, for example) may be open to the charge of incoherence. However underdeveloped Locke's explicit argumentation was, the theological component in his political thought can by no means be set aside as merely a reflection of his having written in a less secular time, a non-essential husk from which the kernel of the Lockean conception of natural rights can be easily extracted. Without the metaphysical doctrines that featured so centrally in the natural law reasoning of Locke's Scholastic predecessors, it is hard to see how he could have any other way of defending the claim that the rights we have derive from the very nature of things, and are not merely the products of a Hobbesian social contract, if he does not ground them in God's ownership of us.

In any event, we can now begin to see why Locke might think that the first of his three conditions on knowledge of the natural law is not the only one that is satisfied. For if we can know that God exists, then since to know this is just to know that there is an omnipotent, omniscient, and omnibenevolent creator (of the universe in general and of us in particular), it follows that we can know, given Locke's view that labor-mixing confers ownership, that we are this divine creator's property. And if we are God's property – evidently created by Him for some purpose or other – it is surely a reasonable assumption that he would want his property to be preserved, in which case it would be a violation of his will for us to kill or maim others, or to steal their property (since the maintenance of their lives depends on their property). Not only can we know that there is a divine lawmaker, then, but we can also plausibly know, to some extent anyway, what his will is.

Still, it isn't clear that this will suffice to tell us *in detail* what rights and obligations we have under the law of nature; in particular, it isn't clear that it suffices to justify belief in the very strong rights to private property and the fruit of one's labor that Locke wants to defend, since these are arguably not essential to one's preservation (though we will return to this question shortly). To justify more specific claims about our rights and obligations would seem to require appealing to a richer conception of human nature than Locke's metaphysics allows. Moreover, as many commentators have noted, there seems to be a serious difficulty for Locke in satisfying his *third* condition for knowledge of the law of nature, viz. that there be knowable sanctions on non-compliance with that law. For though Locke allows that violations of the law of nature often have negative consequences in this life for individuals and society, he denies that such disutility counts as a sanction in the requisite sense, since it "would operate of itself without a law" (E 2.28.6) – that is to say, the negative consequences would often follow even if the law in question were not part of the natural law. A *true* sanction, of the sort required to give a precept the force of law (as opposed to a mere counsel of prudence), must in Locke's view entail that some penalty *be exacted by the lawgiver*. Now since the lawgiver in question in the case of the natural law is God, the requisite sanction would seem to be some punishment in the afterlife for violations of the law of nature committed in this life. This is why it was so important for Locke to defend, in the *Essay*, a theory of personal identity on which life after death is possible. Still, as we saw in our discussion of that theory, Locke's view is that we can know through philosophical argument only that rewards and punishments in the hereafter are *possible*, not that they are actual. But then it would seem that we can have no knowledge of a sanction for violations of the law of nature; and in that case, we can have no knowledge of the purported law of nature as a true *law* at all. Indeed, Locke himself seems in *The Reasonableness of Christianity* to acknowledge that there is a problem here, and even to suggest that our knowledge of morality rests more firmly on biblical revelation than on natural law (RC 197–8).

One way to try to solve the problem, then, might be for Locke to appeal to divine revelation rather than philosophical argument for justification of the claim that there are sanctions in the afterlife for violations of the natural law committed here and now. It might be objected to this that given Locke's account of the nature of revelation, such a justification wouldn't strictly count as *knowledge* in Locke's sense, but at best as justified belief; for a judgment that a revelation has occurred can, on Locke's account, never be more than probable. But this does not seem to be a serious difficulty. After all, given Locke's conception of knowledge, even what we believe about ordinary human laws and penalties for their violation doesn't count as knowledge *per se*, since it doesn't involve either an intuition of the agreement between ideas or demonstrative reasoning. Surely, though, this does not show that our belief in and adherence to such laws is unjustified. Justified belief, rather than knowledge in the Lockean sense, is sufficient in this case. Presumably the "knowledge" required for the law of nature is also better described as justified belief, in which case revelation could in principle provide the needed evidence of sanctions in the hereafter for violations of the natural law occurring in this life.

Tensions with the *Essay*

Nevertheless, as we have seen, Locke is not at all clear about exactly how the belief that a divine revelation has occurred can be justified even as *probably* true if we reject the Catholic appeal to tradition and the Protestant enthusiasts' appeal to personal divine inspiration. Here we have an example of how the epistemological doctrines of the *Essay* seem to pose problems for the moral doctrine of the *Second Treatise*. They pose problems too even for Locke's attempt to satisfy his first condition on knowledge of the law of nature, since as we saw in the previous chapter, even if some versions of the traditional arguments for God's existence are defensible, it seems that Locke's empiricist scruples undermine his own attempt, at least if he is interested (as he must be for the sake of his theory of natural rights) in proving the existence of the creator *ex nihilo* of classical theism. Locke is also sometimes accused of contradicting the *Essay*'s denial of innate ideas in saying, as he does in the *Second Treatise*, that the law of nature is "writ in the hearts of mankind" (T II.11). Here I think he has been read uncharitably, since everything we have seen so far shows that he believed that the foundations of the natural law depend on theistic premises that can be established through philosophical arguments. The statement just quoted is thus surely meant in a loose sense, to the effect that every human being has, by virtue of being rational, the ability to discover and understand the arguments in question. Unfortunately, though, since Locke's epistemology seems in fact to undercut the possibility of such arguments, he has another problem on his hands, one at least as serious as any alleged inconsistency.

There are also tensions between the *Second Treatise* and the metaphysical doctrines of the *Essay*. Locke holds that since we are God's property and thus made for his purposes rather than those of other human beings, we are "equal and independent" and "there cannot be supposed any ... subordination among us" of the sort that exists between us and the lower animals (T II.6). No human being has any natural authority over another, nor any right to use another the way we might use an ox for its labor, for experimentation, or for food. But as Jeremy Waldron has pointed out, a serious difficulty for this egalitarian thesis is posed by the fact that the *Essay* denies that there are any objective species in nature; as we saw in the previous chapter, for Locke, "*the boundaries of the species ... are made by men*; since the essences of the species, distinguished by different names ... are of man's making" (E 3.6.37). It would seem to follow, then, that what counts as a human being, or as a person, is a matter of human convention. We have already seen how some Lockean theorists of personal identity (though not necessarily Locke himself) would deny that fetuses, very young infants, or those in "persistent vegetative states" count as persons. There the reason had to do specifically with the metaphysics of personhood, but here the issue is much more general. If "the boundaries of species are made by men," then it seems it is ultimately up to us to decide not only whether fetuses, PVS patients, and the like count as either human beings or persons, but also whether even the crippled, the stupid, those of other races, and so forth, count as human beings or persons. And in that case, our rights are only as stable as the human conventions that recognize them. Locke tells us that if you are a human being you have certain rights by nature rather than by human fiat, and that no other human being can take them away from you; but he also seems to tell us that what counts as a human being in the first place *is* a matter of human fiat, so that whether you fall into that favored class of rights-bearers is *not* determined by nature. In that case, your rights are just as insecure as they would be if they were not natural at all. What Locke gives you with one hand, he takes back with the other.

Waldron suggests that Locke's solution to this problem is to abandon any appeal to the species "human being" in grounding his doctrine of equal rights, and to focus instead on the characteristic of rationality. "[W]hen we say that 'man is subject to law,'" Locke writes in the *Essay*, "we mean nothing by *man* but a corporeal rational creature: what the real essence or other qualities of that creature are in this case, is no way considered" (E 3.11.16). The "*moral man*," as Locke calls him – a human being considered just as a bearer of moral rights and obligations, and not as a kind of organism – is nothing other than a "*corporeal rational being*" (ibid.). What matters to a particular creature's having natural rights, then, is not whether it falls into the general biological category "human being," but rather whether it possesses the capacity to reason. More precisely, in Waldron's view, what Locke cares about is the "power of *abstracting*" or "the having of general ideas" (E 2.11.10). Why is this the crucial feature? Because, Waldron suggests, the power of abstraction is in Locke's view what gives such creatures "light enough to lead them to the knowledge of their maker" (E 1.1.5) – that is, the ability to reason to the existence of God. As Waldron interprets Locke, his view is that since creatures capable of abstracting can determine that there is a God, that they are his workmanship and therefore his property, and that (given, presumably, Locke's theories of personal identity and free will) they can and will be held accountable by Him for what they do with what he owns, they can know that they must be careful in how they treat what is God's. In particular, they can know that they must be especially careful with respect to *other* creatures capable of knowing this, i.e. other creatures capable of abstract reason. For a creature capable of abstract reason, since it (unlike animals and inanimate objects) can *know* that it is God's creature, is surely under special orders from God (as it were) to do his will, and therefore no other rational creature ought to interfere with the carrying out of those orders. Accordingly in Waldron's view, it is evident that the existence of God is absolutely crucial to Locke's theory of rights, especially when we consider that it is (on Waldron's interpretation) central to his attempt to deal with the problem posed by his denial of the existence of objective species in nature.

The key move here in Waldron's view is Locke's shift away from trying to demarcate the boundaries of the species "human being" to identifying the capacity for reason or abstraction as a morally relevant property. For several reasons, this move seems highly problematic. For one thing, it is hard to see how it really does anything to resolve the basic difficulty facing Locke, for now we need to ask what makes something count as "reason" or "abstraction," and here again we are dealing with species or essences that must in Locke's view be the products of human convention. If it is up to us to determine the boundaries of these categories, then once again any individual's rights would seem ultimately to depend on whether or not we are willing to adopt a convention on which he or she would count as capable of "reasoning" or "abstracting."

In any case, it is not entirely clear exactly why such capacities are so crucial to securing equal rights on a Lockean account. For if talk about "our" rights is really just a kind of shorthand for an imperative to respect *God's* ownership rights over us, why wouldn't the mere fact that we are all owned by God itself suffice to guarantee our equal rights? Of course, this would also seem to entail that everything else that exists – not just human beings, but also animals, and indeed the entire natural world – would have "rights" too by virtue of being God's property, and perhaps it is a desire to avoid this result that motivates the emphasis on reason. But even if this would explain Locke's motive for emphasizing it, it does not in fact seem to provide a convincing justification for that emphasis, since, again, the appeal to God's ownership of us would seem all by itself to entail Lockean rights. Why should it matter whether something God owns is capable of *knowing* that it is owned by Him? Shouldn't God's property rights in unthinking things be respected no less than his rights over everything else? (Your car doesn't know you own it, but that doesn't mean I don't have a duty not to steal it.) Moreover, the emphasis on reason and abstraction would seem to imply that human beings who are not in fact capable of these things – the mentally retarded, the demented, fetuses, and perhaps even infants and young children – would not have rights of the sort Locke wants to attribute to us. Surely a Christian thinker like Locke would be troubled by the thought that his account might have such a consequence.

As we noted earlier, such a consequence would have been ruled out by the Scholastics by appealing to the soul or substantial form that all human beings instantiate in (however imperfectly) simply by virtue of being human as guaranteeing personhood and the rights that go along with it. And the later Scholastic theories of natural rights, tied as they were to the natural ends unique to creatures capable of moral reflection and responsibility, would similarly have ruled out the possibility that animals or the natural world in general could meaningfully be said to have rights. It is interesting that Locke's abandonment of the Scholastic notions of substantial forms and natural ends should arguably have as a consequence (even if he did not intend this) the possibility of attributing "rights" of a sort to non-human animals and the environment and the denial of rights to at least some human beings, such as fetuses and the severely mentally impaired – consequences that some contemporary philosophers, whose metaphysical views are in many respects descended from those of Locke, are quite happy to endorse. Of course, as Waldron would emphasize, the existence of *any* rights (including the purported rights of animals and the like) must, on a Lockean view, presuppose the existence of God as the owner of the earth and its inhabitants, and this is a presupposition most of the contemporary philosophers in question are unwilling to endorse. But it is nevertheless hard to believe that it could be accidental that when you follow through consistently the implications of Locke's metaphysics, his own conception of rights seems in many ways to transform into something resembling these contemporary views.

This is a topic we will have reason to return to later. For now let us note one further respect in which Locke's metaphysics might pose difficulties for his political philosophy. We have seen that for Locke, personal identity is not, as it was for the Scholastics, tied to the having of a particular human body, since he takes it to be at least conceptually possible that one and the same person could move from one body to an entirely different one, as in his example of the prince and the cobbler. Personhood, for Locke, resides entirely in the continuity of one's consciousness. But in that case, it seems to follow that one's body is, strictly speaking, something external to and distinct from one's self. You are your consciousness, and your body is merely something your consciousness happens, contingently, to inhabit, just as you might inhabit a house or a car. It is no more a part of you than the house or car is. Now if this is true, then it would also seem to follow that a human body can reasonably be regarded as an external natural resource alongside other resources, such as food, water, and the raw materials out of which we build tools, houses, and the other things we need in order to survive. And in that case, it isn't clear why we shouldn't suppose it possible that someone else could come to acquire ownership rights in your body before your consciousness comes to inhabit it, by "mixing" his or her labor with it *à la* Lockean theory of property. In particular, it isn't clear why your parents couldn't claim ownership rights over your body by virtue of having created and nourished it long before you developed any capacity for consciousness or rationality. But if they could claim such ownership rights, then they – or someone else who has acquired rights to your body (perhaps by buying those rights from your parents) – could also put any number of restrictions on how you use that body, even after you have become an adult, just as the owner of a house or apartment can put restrictions on how anyone who rents it may use it.

Obviously this is a consequence Locke would not be happy with (especially given that, in arguing against Filmer, he explicitly rejects the view that parents can own their children – see chapter 6 of the *First Treatise*). It seems to make vacuous the very idea of self-ownership; for what you own by virtue of being a self-owner would seem to be merely your stream of consciousness, and not the body that that consciousness inhabits, in which case even someone who denied you the right to use that body in the ways you wanted to would not necessarily thereby be violating your self-ownership rights. Now as we will see, Locke does put certain restrictions on the acquisition of property that entail that no one's property rights can ever be so strong as to allow people to starve to death who, through no fault of their own, were unable to acquire property of their own. So it is plausible to suppose that even if someone other than you could come to own your body, he or she would at least have to allow you to use it in a way that made it possible for you to keep yourself – that is to say, your stream of consciousness – in existence as long as you could. But that is nevertheless consistent with someone else – including, in principle, the government – coming to have so much control over what you can do with your body that your condition would be little better than that of a slave. Locke's entire theory of natural rights thus seems threatened by his theory of personal identity. If the person who has the rights is really just a (potentially disembodied) stream of consciousness, then the rights he or she has by virtue of being a self-owner are not rights over any part of the material world with which we need to interact in order to be free in any meaningful sense.

Private property

Whatever one thinks of this potential problem for Locke's theory, it brings us back to his account of property, which we now want to examine in more detail. Let us begin by reminding ourselves of the overall theory of natural law and natural rights in which that account is embedded. Human beings, Locke says, are God's "workmanship" and therefore his property, "sent into the world by his order, and about his business." From this fact we can derive the "fundamental law of nature," which is that human beings must be preserved as much as possible, so as to respect God's property rights. This entails in turn several derivative laws of nature, such as that no one may harm another in his "life, health, liberty or possessions." And these laws together imply that we ought to treat other human beings as if they were self-owners, having a "property in their own persons," at least relative to each other (even though they are not self-owners relative to God). These self-ownership rights comprise the natural rights we have by virtue of being human beings, or at least by virtue of being rational creatures.

Now the reference above to "possessions" indicates that Locke regards the right to private property as in some sense a natural right. But that is not because he thinks that there is any specific part of the natural world that any individual is born having a right to. Indeed, Locke says that "God gave the world to men in common" (T II.34), because all human beings "have a right to their preservation, and consequently to meat and drink, and such other things as nature affords for their subsistence" (T II.25). The reason natural resources exist, in other words, is for human beings to preserve themselves so that they may carry out their duties to God. So in some sense every human being has a right to the use of those resources. Still, this obviously does not mean that in Locke's view there can be no such thing as private property. On the contrary, Locke thinks that the legitimacy of private property is entailed by the fact that the earth exists for our subsistence, together with the thesis that we are all self-owners.

How so? The first thing to note is that the fact that God gave the earth to all human beings in common for their subsistence cannot in Locke's view be interpreted to mean that we all collectively own the earth in a sense that would require that any individual has to get the consent of every other human being before he or she can take possession of some particular resource. For it is, of course, impossible for anyone to get such consent, both because no one can possibly consult every other human being before picking an apple or building a house, and because even if someone could do this, there might be some other people who would refuse to give their consent. Thus, "if such a consent as that was necessary, man had starved, notwithstanding the plenty God had given him" (T II.28). The whole point of the resources existing in the first place – the sustenance of human life – would be defeated, because in practice no one would ever be able to use them if the consent of everyone else was necessary. So God's gift of the earth to all of us in common does not entail, in Locke's view, any kind of communistic view to the effect that we all collectively share ownership of natural resources. Rather, it seems in his view to entail that, at least initially, *no* human beings either individually or collectively own any resources at all, that "nobody has originally a private dominion, exclusive of the rest of mankind, in any of them, as they are thus in their natural state" (T II.26). All the earth's resources are, at the start anyway, "up for grabs" (subject, as we will see, to certain conditions).

This is where self-ownership comes in, as the key to explaining how an individual can come to appropriate a part of the earth's resources for his or her own use. As Locke puts it in a famous passage:

> Though the earth, and all inferior creatures, be common to all men, yet every man has a property in his own person: this nobody has any right to but himself. The labour of his body, and the work of his hands, we may say, are properly his. Whatsoever then he removes out of the state that nature hath provided, and left it in, he hath mixed his labour with, and joined to it something that is his own, and thereby makes it his property. It being by him removed from the common state nature hath placed it in, it hath by this labour something annexed to it that excludes the common right of other men. For this labour being the unquestionable property of the labourer, no man but he can have a right to what that is once joined to. (T II.27)

In short, if no one in particular initially owns some particular resource, and you come along and "mix your labor" with that resource, you thereby become the first to have a property right in it, because you have now put into it something that you did already own. Anyone who would take that resource from you without your consent would thereby be violating your rights, because in effect he or she would in that case be stealing your labor from you, which is yours by virtue of your being a self-owner.

To reinforce this point, Locke notes that natural resources are useful to us only because they can be transformed, through our labor, into something valuable; by themselves they actually have little value:

> [I]t is labour indeed that put the difference of value on every thing; and let any one consider what the difference is between an acre of land planted with tobacco or sugar, sown with wheat or barley, and an acre of the same land lying in common, without any husbandry upon it, and he will find, that the improvement of labour makes the far greater part of the value. (T II.40)

Indeed, Locke estimates that "nine-tenths" or even "ninety-nine hundredths" of the value of resources "are wholly to be put on the account of labour" (ibid.). To take without someone else's consent the resources he or she has acquired through the use of labor, then, is in the standard case to benefit from value that he or she is almost entirely responsible for putting into them. That one would in that case effectively be stealing someone else's labor is thereby made more manifest.

Now there are limits, in Locke's view, to how much property one can acquire in this way, at least in primitive economic conditions where money does not yet exist. "The same law of nature, that does by this means give us property, does also bound that property too" (T II.31). Specifically, there are what commentators on Locke often identify as two "provisos" he puts on the appropriation of previously unowned resources. First, since "nothing was made by God for man to spoil or destroy," no one can legitimately acquire a resource that he cannot use before it spoils, and anything he does so acquire "is more than his share, and belongs to others" (T II.31). Second, one must leave "enough, and as good, left in common for others" (T II.27; see also T II.33). Since the earth's resources exist in order for human beings to sustain themselves, no one can justifiably take so much for himself that others are left with nothing to acquire for themselves, and thus no way to subsist. So if you take some water from a river, enclose a parcel of land, or gather some fruit for your family that will all be eaten, no one can legitimately complain about this if there is plenty more water, land, and fruit for others to acquire. But if you take all the arable land in a region for yourself or monopolize the only source of fresh water, or take tons of fruit that is bound to spoil before you can eat it, then you have – given the very point for which such resources exist – taken more than you can have a right to, and others have a right to complain and to prevent you from keeping all of these resources. Even though no one in particular has a right to any specific resource before someone mixes his or her labor with it, we all have at least a very general right to acquire some resources or other for ourselves so as to sustain ourselves. This follows from the fundamental law of nature – to preserve mankind as much as possible – which in turn follows from our duty to make sure that God's property (namely ourselves) is not damaged and can fulfill the purposes for which he made it.

As indicated, though, these provisos really only have direct application, in Locke's view, prior to the invention of money. Money comes into being because a barter economy is incredibly inefficient. If you have more wheat than you can use but lack honey, which you do want, someone nearby has plenty of honey but wants beef instead of wheat in return for it, and a third person several miles away has beef to trade but wants wheat rather than honey in exchange, then the three of you will have to find out about each other and arrange some way to meet and engage in a three-way transaction that will satisfy everyone. This is enough of a nuisance, but when we imagine that in a real world situation it is unlikely that you'll always be able to find just the right set of people to agree to such a complicated set of exchanges, and consider a scenario involving hundreds, thousands, or millions of people with hundreds of thousands of different possible goods and services to exchange, it becomes clear that in a barter economy it would be impossible to sustain human beings at much more than a subsistence level of existence. Some common medium of exchange, something that everyone will be willing to take in return for any given good or service, is crucial if a higher standard of living for everyone is going to be possible. Money also opens the door to the possibility of significant profits for those with goods or services to sell, which motivates people to try to be the ones consumers go to in order to get the goods and services they want, i.e. to provide the supply of what people demand. This facilitates specialization and a division of labor, as each agent in the marketplace tries to focus on providing those specific goods or services that he or she is personally best suited to producing, and it also generates new technologies and other innovations, as producers try to foresee consumer needs and open up new markets. And since those producers who are best able to satisfy consumer demands are going to be the ones who prosper the most in the marketplace, there is, all things being equal, an incentive to keep quality relatively high and prices relatively low so as to attract as many customers as possible.

All in all, the institution of money and the market economy it makes possible create a set of economic circumstances that are vastly improved compared to the primitive subsistence conditions that would have prevailed when human beings were first acquiring raw natural resources by mixing their labor with them. This seems to entail, in Locke's view, that the proviso to leave "enough and as good for others" becomes otiose, because the point of that proviso was just to guarantee that people would be able to sustain themselves in existence, and they are far better able to do that, and at a higher standard of living, in a money and market economy than in a primitive barter economy. That the average citizen of a modern capitalist country cannot easily find virgin land to be the first to acquire thus hardly means that he or she is unable to find food, clothing, or shelter, even if doing so requires working for someone else who owns land and other raw materials. Moreover, since money doesn't spoil, one does not violate the spoilage proviso by accumulating even vast amounts of it: "gold and silver ... may be hoarded up without injury to anyone; these metals not spoiling or decaying in the hands of the possessor" (T II.50). That this would result in inequalities is irrelevant, since anyone "might heap as much of these durable things as he pleased; the exceeding of the bounds of his just property not lying in the largeness of his possession, but the perishing of any thing uselessly in it" (T II.46). The law of nature requires not economic equality *per se*, but merely that people be able to sustain themselves through their labor, even if only at a subsistence level. So as long as this is possible, and no one spoils or destroys the resources God has provided, no violation of that law has been committed.

In any event, citizens of a money- and market-based society have no basis for complaining about it, Locke says, because they inhabit it by "tacit and voluntary consent" (T II.50). This might seem implausible at first glance, for there are certainly people living in modern capitalist societies who claim that they would prefer living in some other kind of society. But on reflection Locke seems right. It is, after all, still possible to live the way people lived before money was invented. It is just so extremely difficult to live that way that very few people choose to do it. Indeed, few critics of modern capitalist society have ever actually tried to leave it – by emigrating to a communist country, say, or by starting a commune or becoming a "survivalist" – and the few who do try tend to give up on the experiment before long. In fact, it is probably fair to say that far more people are trying to get *into* capitalist countries every year (indeed, every day) than have ever tried to get out of them. At the end of the day, then, to judge from the way people "vote with their feet," Locke is correct to say that most members of modern money- and market-based societies have tacitly consented to live in them. Even if they might occasionally complain about those societies, they show by their actions that they either cannot envision, or are unwilling to try to create, any alternative system.

This does not mean, however, that Locke was a *laissez faire* libertarian of the Robert Nozick stripe, who would deny that there is necessarily any injustice suffered by those who fail to support themselves in the marketplace. For he does seem to acknowledge that those who, through no fault of their own, are unable to sustain themselves with their labor in a money-based economy can rightfully demand assistance from those who are able so to sustain themselves. In the *First Treatise* he writes:

> But we know God hath not left one man so to the mercy of another, that he may starve him if he please: God, the Lord and Father of all, has given no one of his children such a property in his peculiar portion of the things of this world, but that he has given his needy brother a right to the surplusage of his goods; so that it cannot justly be denied him, when his pressing wants call for it: and therefore no man could ever have a just power over the life of another by right of property in land or possessions; since it would always be a sin, in any man of estate, to let his brother perish for want of affording him relief out of his plenty. As justice gives every man a title to the product of his honest industry, and the fair acquisitions of his ancestors descended to him; so charity gives every man a title to so much out of another's plenty as will keep him from extreme want, where he has no means to subsist otherwise. (T I.42)

This would seem to entail, say, the legitimacy in principle of at least a minimum level of unemployment insurance provided by government and funded by taxation. A libertarian reader of Locke might latch on to the reference to "charity" in the last sentence and argue that Locke is not really saying that government can justifiably force people to fund such public assistance, but only that it would be uncharitable (but not unjust) for us to refuse voluntarily to help those desperately in need. Yet Locke does not just say that we ought to help such people out of charity; he says they have "a *right*" to such assistance, and that "it cannot *justly* be denied" them. If it is a matter of respecting their rights and the demands of justice, then, it is hard to see why government could not legitimately provide such a "safety net." More to the point, that such a safety net is justifiable seems clearly to follow from Locke's overall theory of property. Since the reason God gave the earth to human beings was to allow all of them, as far as possible, to sustain themselves through their labor, it would make no sense to suppose that people could form such strong property rights to the resources they acquire that it could be just for them (even if uncharitable) to allow people to starve who simply never had the chance to acquire any resources of their own with which to sustain themselves. Just as, prior to the invention of money, a proviso exists to ensure that we leave others "enough and as good" natural resources for themselves to acquire, so too, after the invention of money, those who do not own property have a right to assistance when circumstances prevent them from supporting themselves with their labor in a complex market economy.

Locke's position, then, is not Nozick's: he does not insist that any government assistance to the needy necessarily involves violating the property rights of the citizens who pay taxes in order to fund such assistance. The reason is that, given the very point for which private property exists, no one's property rights can possibly be so strong as to rule out such taxation. Still, the only sort of redistributive measure he does appear explicitly to advocate, and in any case the only one that his account of property seems to support, is provision for those who are destitute through no fault of their own. For it isn't clear how such provision would be justifiable, on a Lockean view, for those whose poverty results from their own laziness or folly. Locke says that "God gave the world ... to the use of the industrious and rational ... not to the fancy or covetousness of the quarrelsome and contentious" (T II.34). It would therefore seem to follow, in Locke's view, that those whose inability to support themselves derives from their own failures of industry and rationality can have no claim against those who have surplus resources, for their poverty does not in fact stem from their lack of resources to acquire for themselves. Presumably they would have been poor even if they had such resources, for they would in that case still have lacked the wisdom and/or work ethic to use them properly. There would thus seem to be nothing in Locke's "enough and as good" proviso (or in any analogue to that proviso applying in the context of a money economy) that could justify redistribution, to those who are idle, of the surplus of others, at least not as a matter of justice. Indeed, Locke's explicit statements about how such people ought to be treated are far from sympathetic. In "An Essay on the Poor Law," he advocates hard labor, whipping, and the like for those "idle vagabonds" who merely "pretend they cannot get work" (EPL 184–5).

In general, he says in the same essay, "the true and proper relief of the poor ... consists in finding work for them, and taking care they do not live like drones upon the labour of others" (EPL 189). Even the deserving poor, then, would seem in his view to be entitled only to that measure of assistance they need until such time as they can become self-sufficient. We have also already seen that Locke has no objection to inequality as such. Nor is there anything in his theory of property that would justify government provision of health care, social security, or a general redistribution of wealth for the purposes of trying to realize some egalitarian pattern of income distribution. Indeed, Locke would surely have held, as Nozick does, that for government to attempt to perform these functions via taxation would be unjust, a violation of taxpayers' property rights. So while Locke is no libertarian, it is also clear that he is not an egalitarian liberal of the John Rawls stripe or an advocate of what today would be called "the welfare state."

It is also worth emphasizing that even the modest redistributive component of Locke's theory seems to depend entirely on the assumption that God gave the earth and its resources to human beings for their common use in sustaining themselves. If one eliminates this theological assumption – as most contemporary liberals and libertarians would – then it seems that Locke's view would revert to a radically libertarian one. For if not even God initially owns the earth and its resources, and neither God nor anyone else ever gave those resources to mankind in common for their sustenance (or for any other purpose for that matter), then it seems that Locke's provisos on the initial acquisition of natural resources, and his apparent defense of something like a kind of unemployment insurance in the context of a money economy, lack any philosophical foundation. Natural resources would in that case start out not being owned by anyone, and would serve no natural purpose, so that if some people were just lucky enough to acquire all the resources for themselves, or decided to waste them, it is hard to see how they could be said to be acting unjustly. For whose rights would they be violating in that case? Not God's, because by hypothesis he doesn't exist. Nor any other human being's rights either, because by hypothesis no human being had any claim over those resources in the first place, given that they started out unowned by anyone. Nor could a would-be atheistic Lockean appeal in quasi-Aristotelian fashion to the natural ends or functions of human labor and/or of natural resources as a way of shoring up the claim that all human beings have a right to the use of the earth's resources, since Locke rejects all such Aristotelian notions. If there is no God who gives us the earth in common for our sustenance, then, it seems that Locke would have no basis for putting limits on the acquisition of property. Here as elsewhere, Locke's political philosophy depends crucially on its theological assumptions.

In any event, Locke's theory of property has been controversial even apart from its theological commitments. Probably the most common criticisms are directed at the idea that "mixing" one's labor with unowned natural resources suffices to generate a property right in them. As Nozick, who otherwise sympathizes with Locke's account, has famously asked:

> Why does mixing one's labor with something make one the owner of it? ... [W]hy isn't mixing what I own with what I don't own a way of losing what I own rather than a way of gaining what I don't? If I

own a can of tomato juice and spill it in the sea so that its molecules (made radioactive, so I can check this) mingle evenly throughout the sea, do I thereby come to own the sea, or have I foolishly dissipated my tomato juice?

This particular objection does not seem to be fatal. For while there are certainly cases, like the one Nozick mentions, where mixing one thing with another entails the disappearance of the first thing, there are also clear cases where this does not happen, as when one pours one's tomato juice into a glass of vodka to make a Bloody Mary. Surely Locke could plausibly hold that while there are instances where one's labor is simply dissipated and fails to confer ownership, there are also obvious cases where it is not dissipated. For example, someone who merely blows gently in the direction of a piece of driftwood floating by does not plausibly thereby come to own it, but someone who takes it and carves it into a statuette or a walking stick does plausibly come to own it. So perhaps it would suffice to answer Nozick's objection if Locke were to specify that it is labor that results in a significant degree of *control* over a resource that confers ownership.

One could still ask, however, why even labor that is not dissipated or ineffective should be seen as conferring ownership. True, if I take a piece of previously unowned driftwood and carve it into a statuette, my labor has not been wasted in the way Nozick's tomato juice was, insofar as I have dramatically altered the driftwood and created something new and perhaps even valuable. But how precisely does this show that I thereby have generated a property right in the statuette? To borrow an example from Waldron, suppose I drop a diamond that I own into a vat of wet cement that no one owns, and the cement hardens. Here there is no question of the diamond being destroyed or dissipated, as in the tomato juice example: it is perfectly intact, even if now inaccessible. Still, how would this show that I have thereby come to *own* the cement? The point doesn't hinge on whether or not I could justifiably break open the cement to get the diamond back out; for even supposing I could legitimately do this, how would the mere presence of my diamond in the cement give me rights of *ownership* over it?

Here, as Waldron points out, the "teleology" or purpose of natural resources and labor is crucial to Locke's account. There is a connection between labor and natural resources that just doesn't exist between diamonds and cement or tomato juice and the sea, for God has in Locke's view given us natural resources precisely for the purpose of laboring on them. Yet again Locke's theological premises are indispensable.

It isn't clear that even these premises will suffice to solve the problem for Locke, however. For given his rejection of Aristotelian natural ends and functions, it is hard to see how Locke could justify the claim that labor and resources have any purpose or "teleology" at all. Appeal to God's intentions won't help, because unless Locke wants to claim that God has given us some revelation explicitly telling us what labor and natural resources are for – and Locke does not in fact rest his argument on such a claim – then he will have to try to "read off" God's intentions from observation of the natural world, and there is no way he can do this if he rejects natural ends and functions of the Scholastic or Aristotelian sort. Moreover, what *counts* as "labor" or as a "natural resource" must, for Locke, ultimately be a matter of human convention anyway, since all species and essences are conventional on his view; and it is hardly plausible to suppose that a consideration of concepts that reflect nothing but human interests might reveal to us the divine will. (Other aspects of Locke's theory of property seem to face similar difficulties. For instance, the "spoilage" proviso presupposes that we can know what counts as wasting a natural resource, and it is difficult to see how we could know this without knowing the objective natural end or function a resource serves.)

From the state of nature to civil society

Our rights to our property, like our rights in general, are in Locke's view "natural" to us in the sense that they are not the products of human convention or agreement. Rather, they precede all conventions and agreements and place stringent moral constraints on what conventions and agreements we can legitimately adopt. Here Locke firmly opposes Hobbes, who thinks that we have "rights" in the state of nature only in the sense that there are no binding moral limits on our actions so that we have the "right" to do whatever we want to do, period. For Hobbes, it is because of the chaos and violence this entails that people mutually agree to leave the state of nature, and to guarantee their safety by submitting themselves to an all-powerful sovereign. Morality arises out of this mutual agreement, and its rules are just whatever rules the various parties to the contract have agreed to follow. For Locke, by contrast, morality already exists in the state of nature, with everyone having a genuine obligation to respect everyone else's rights to their lives, health, liberty, and possessions even before civil society and government come into being. The "social contract" that creates civil society and government does not create morality itself, and it must be consistent with the rules of morality.

While in the state of nature, people have what Locke calls the "executive power of the law of nature" (T II.13); that is to say, they have the moral right to defend their own rights and the rights of others, including a right to punish those who violate people's rights. The reason, Locke says, is that unless people in the state of nature had the right to defend their rights, "the law of nature would ... be in vain" (T II.7), insofar as in that case there would be no way to enforce it. Now if the state of nature is governed by morality, and those living in it have the right to defend themselves, why would people agree to leave it? What desire or need would there be for government? The answer is that while the state of nature is not, for Locke, nearly as bad as it is for Hobbes, it nevertheless has certain "inconveniencies" (T II.127). The first is that people sometimes differ in their interpretations of what the law of nature requires, and thus will often disagree about whether someone's rights have truly been violated, especially given the bias we all have in our own favor (T II.124). Secondly, this bias will also often lead people to inflict excessive punishments in retaliation for offenses committed against them (T II.125). Thirdly, even though all individuals in the state of nature have a moral right to defend their rights, many of them will lack the power to do so and find themselves at the mercy of stronger aggressors (T II.126). Those in the state of nature will, therefore, have reason to seek a single impartial interpreter and enforcer of the law of nature, which is why they decide to leave the state of nature and establish civil society and government.

This happens in the following stages. First, individuals consent to "[put] an end to the state of nature between men" by "agreeing together mutually to enter into one community, and make one body politic" (T II.14). In doing so, they divest themselves of their right to enforce the law of nature, having "resigned it up into the hands of the community" (T II.87). The enforcement of everyone's natural rights now becomes a public and collective matter, with "all private judgment of every particular member being excluded" (ibid.). This entails in Locke's view that anyone who exits the state of nature to form the community "puts himself under an obligation to everyone of that society to submit to the determination of the majority, and to be concluded by it" (T II.97). For:

> that which acts any community being only the consent of the individuals of it, and it being necessary to that which is one body to move one way; it is necessary the body should move that way whither the greater force carries it, which is the consent of the majority: or else it is impossible it should act or continue one body, one community, which the consent of every individual that united into it agreed that it should. (T II.96)

In short, since there is no way for a community to act collectively at all except by following the will of the majority of its members, to agree to enter into a community is *ipso facto* to agree to abide by the will of the majority.

Lest there be any misunderstanding, it is crucial to understand that Locke is *not* here claiming that democracy is the only legitimate form of government, or even trying to defend it at all. For by "the community" Locke does not mean any particular real world society or form of government in the first place. What he has in mind is something more abstract than that. The "community" is just a group of individuals who have decided to leave the state of nature, and which has therefore taken it upon itself to choose some form of government to live under. The specific form they choose will be decided by the majority of the community, but it could well be that what the majority decides upon is a non-democratic form of government, such as a constitutional monarchy or some other form of government that does not involve allowing the mass of citizens to vote on who will hold office or on what specific policies should be followed.

Nevertheless, the community cannot do just whatever it likes. In particular, it could not legitimately decide upon a *tyrannical* form of government, since the whole point of leaving the state of nature is to guarantee the effective enforcement of every individual's natural rights. This is one reason it is important for Locke's overall political philosophy that individuals do not have the right to commit suicide or to sell themselves into slavery; for while we can legitimately give up to the community, and thus to government, rights that we ourselves possess – such as the right to enforce the law of nature – we cannot give up to it rights we do not possess, such as the right to give up our own lives or liberty. "Nobody can give more power than he has himself," Locke writes, "and he that cannot take away his own life, cannot give another power over it" (T II.23). The prohibition on suicide, etc., is thus motivated not only by a desire to respect God's rights over us, but also to block the possibility of the community deciding upon a form of government that had unlimited power over its citizens. What might seem to the modern libertarian to be a restriction on freedom is in fact intended as a bulwark against Hobbesian absolutism.

Once the community agrees to a particular form of government, and its members therefore have "a common established law and judicature to appeal to, with authority to decide controversies between them, and punish offenders," they are "in civil society one with another" (T II.87). The form of government they have chosen will then go on to be implemented by whatever particular administration holds power at any given moment, where this administration will give way to another according to the rules enshrined in the form of government – via periodic elections, say, or by one monarch being succeeded upon his or her death by an heir. The transition from the state of nature to ordinary everyday life in civil society is thus not direct. Individuals first agree to form the community, then the community chooses a specific form of government, and finally a particular administration holds power. It is only the first stage that involves the direct consent of every single individual, with the second stage requiring only a majority decision, and the third stage not necessarily requiring even that if the form of government chosen by the community is non-democratic. It is also only at the first stage that we have a "social contract," which on Locke's theory is a contract between those individuals who decide to leave the state of nature and form a community, not a contract between citizens and those who happen to hold power at a particular time. A government instead holds power on "trust" from the community (T II.149), acting as the community's agent rather than as a partner to a contract, where a contract might imply that the government has rights against the people just as the people have rights against it. It is, in Locke's view, in fact only the people who have rights against government, and not the other way round.

Locke says that the "consent" of individuals to leave the state of nature and form a community "is that, and that only, which did or could give beginning to any lawful government in the world" (T II.99). One might naturally object to this that in reality people have rarely, if ever, actually formed a society in this way, viz. by starting from scratch in a state of nature and explicitly agreeing to form a community which goes on to choose a particular form of government. But Locke's reply to such an objection is to argue that "every man, that hath any possessions, or enjoyment of any part of the dominions of any government, doth thereby give his tacit consent, and is as far forth obliged to obedience to the laws of that government, during such enjoyment, as any one under it" (T II.119). Just as those who participate in a money economy tacitly consent to it, so too do those who abide within a certain territory and accept the services of its government tacitly consent to that government. It is *as if* they had expressly left the state of nature and joined a community which decided upon that government.

It should be noted that there is nothing in this that implies that Locke thinks that those who live under a tyrannical government and accept its services have thereby consented to it and have no right to complain. For though Locke certainly thinks consent is a necessary condition for a legitimate government – he says that "no one can be ... subjected to the political power of another, without his own consent" (T II.95) – he does not think it is a sufficient condition. Government exists in order to defend its citizens' natural rights, and any government that fails to do this therefore cannot be legitimate. So it would seem that what Locke really wants to say is that if a government more or less respects and defends its citizens' rights – including, say, a right to emigrate if one wishes to – and a person continues to dwell within its territory and accepts its services, then that person has tacitly consented to it.

Still, as with Locke's appeal to tacit consent in defending the money economy, it might seem implausible to suggest that everyone even in contemporary liberal and democratic societies has tacitly consented to live within them. Don't many people complain about the democratic governments they live under, and sometimes complain even about the liberal democratic political system itself? Is their failure to emigrate really a sign that they have tacitly consented, given that emigration can be extremely difficult and that any other democratic country they could hope to move to would likely have just the same problems as the one they left? Here too, though, it isn't clear that such objections to Locke are really all that impressive. As noted before, it is still possible even in this day and age to live the life of a hermit or a survivalist, even if few people choose to do so. True, this would be a very difficult sort of life to live, but it wouldn't be any more difficult than life in the state of nature. Furthermore, to opt to leave the state of nature at all is, as Locke argues, to opt to abide by the decisions of the majority of one's fellow members of the community. And if most members of the community think the existing government is legitimate – as probably the vast majority of the citizens of existing liberal democratic governments do – then one has to go along with their decision if one wants to leave the state of nature. In short, Locke could say to the would-be anarchist that his or her continued participation in a society that more or less respects its citizens' natural rights (or at least does so as well as any other existing government does), and most of whose members regard it as legitimate, constitutes tacit consent to the government of that society, since someone who was really so opposed to it that he or she would prefer living in the state of nature (so as to avoid having to go along with the majority of the community) could always take up the life of a survivalist. Having complaints, even reasonable ones, about the existing order just doesn't suffice to show that one hasn't tacitly consented to that order. Perfection isn't possible, and while even the best real world government is bound to have significant flaws, surely life in the state of nature would be worse. If the flaws in some government aren't big enough to lead someone living under it to take radical steps to escape it, then, it is not unreasonable to suggest that that person has tacitly accepted it as the best option practically available if he or she wants to leave the state of nature and participate in civil society at all.

Of course, this just raises the question of exactly *how* flawed a government can get before it no longer counts as fulfilling Locke's condition that a legitimate government is one which is not only consented to, but which respects and defends its citizens' rights. Obviously a government of the sort run by a Hitler or a Stalin has crossed the line, and would lose legitimacy even if a majority of the citizens supported it, since it would so unmistakably violate individual rights to life, liberty, and property. But what about a society which is founded on broadly Lockean principles, as the United States is, but whose government is nevertheless arguably flawed from a Lockean point of view – insofar as, for example, it taxes its citizens at a much higher rate than Locke would presumably allow, so as to fund a welfare state that goes far beyond the modest relief for the poor that he envisioned? Could a contemporary libertarian inspired by Locke reasonably declare such a government illegitimate, whether or not his or her fellow citizens consent to live under it? Not necessarily. Recall that while Locke thinks that certain things are clearly contrary to our natural rights, such as killing or enslaving an innocent person, he also says that people differ in their interpretations of the details of what the law of nature requires. This is one of the "inconveniencies" of the state of nature, and why government and civil society are needed in Locke's view to provide "an established, settled, known law, received and allowed by common consent to be the standard of right and wrong, and the common measure to decide all controversies" (T II.124). That a particular citizen might plausibly argue that some particular government programs are unjustifiable from a Lockean point of view would, therefore, not seem by itself sufficient to show that the government is illegitimate, since there seems to be enough ambiguity in the law of nature, on Locke's account, that reasonable people might disagree over how to apply it.

Moreover, since in Locke's view to join the community at all is to agree to consent to the form of government endorsed by the majority, if the majority of the people reasonably consider some particular programs as a plausible application of the fundamental law of nature, then even if they happen to be mistaken one would have to agree to tolerate their decision. And we should remember too that Locke takes the "fundamental law of nature" to be "that all, as much as may be, should be preserved," and holds that this entails certain limitations on private property rights. Surely it is not *obviously* wrongheaded to think that these premises might be used as a basis for a defense of the modern welfare state so opposed by libertarians. Of course, people who tried to give such a defense might in fact be mistaken (and, for what it is worth, I myself think they would be mistaken), but that is beside the point. As long as an interpretation of the Lockean law of nature along "big government" lines is at least a reasonable possibility, a more libertarian Lockean couldn't condemn as inherently unjust a society the majority of whose members decide to opt for that interpretation. he or she could, of course, try to convince the majority that it is mistaken in its interpretation of the law of nature, and work within the system to try to correct the flaws he or she sees in it. But such a libertarian could not plausibly conclude, on Lockean grounds anyway, that the government in question was just flatly illegitimate and unworthy of allegiance.

Even if we allowed that Locke is correct to hold that (at least tacit) consent is sufficient to confer legitimacy on a government that more or less respects and defends the rights of its citizens, we might still question whether Locke is right to say that such consent is necessary. For suppose that the majority of some group of people in the state of nature decide not to leave it to form a community or establish a government. And suppose further that while most of these people are able to defend their rights on their own, some of them – widows, the elderly, orphans, or whoever – are too weak to do so and are constantly under threat from stronger aggressors. Would this be a just situation? It seems that Locke would have to say that it would be. Of course, he would condemn as unjust the actions of the individual aggressors, but there would seem, from a Lockean point of view, to be no injustice over and above those specific actions. In particular, there would be no injustice committed by the other members of the group in refusing to come together to form a government that would protect the rights of the weak as well as of the strong. But this would seem to be in tension with Locke's claim that the fundamental law of nature requires us to preserve human beings as far as possible. Respecting that fundamental law would seem to entail that a group such as the one in question *must* establish a government that would defend everyone's rights, even if they do not want to do so. And it thereby seems to entail that, given that such a government really does defend its citizens' natural rights, the consent of the people is not necessary to give it legitimacy. The law of nature seems all by itself to call forth government as a guarantor of *everyone's* rights – not just the rights of the strong.

Now this raises the question of what would constitute such a group of people *as* a group (to be distinguished from other groups) in the first place. And related to this is the question of what distinguishes one "community," in Locke's sense, from another. Why, on a Lockean view, should we count the members of a particular country – the United States, say, or Switzerland, or France – as members of a single "community"? Why not instead count them as comprising a collection of communities (Californians, Texans, Alaskans, etc., or even New Yorkers, Bostonians, and Chicagoans)? Or why not instead count the French speakers who live in Switzerland, together with those in France and Quebec, as one big gerrymandered community, with those Swiss who speak Italian being part of the same community as other Italian speakers, and so forth – so that "Switzerland" doesn't really name a single community but rather parts of various communities? Indeed, why not consider *any* given way of dividing individuals into classes – by family ties, or religious affiliation, or even by hobbies – as marking the boundaries of a Lockean "community"? Why couldn't any group of people, however scattered across the globe and defined by whatever common attribute, plausibly regard themselves as comprising a "community" which ought to be allowed to form its own governmental structures, regardless of whatever existing governments might claim their respective allegiances? By the same token, why couldn't any individual regard himself or herself as *not* being a member of the community he or she is surrounded by, and therefore as neither a party to its social contract nor (for that reason) subject to the laws of its government? For instance (and to take some real world examples), why couldn't a corporate executive living in the United States see his true allegiance as belonging to the global corporation of which he is a part rather than to the American government, and why couldn't a radical Islamist living in the United Kingdom see his allegiance as rightly belonging to the worldwide Islamic community rather than to the British government? Locke's talk of the "community" presupposes that we have some way of identifying it, but he gives us no guidance as to *how*, specifically, we should identify it.

Both of these potential problems for Locke's account – the problem of how the rights of the weak could be defended if a particular group of people do not consent to form a community, and the problem of what demarcates such a group or community in the first place – arguably derive from the same source, namely the individualism Locke shares with the broad liberal political tradition of which he is a part. The tendency of individualism is to regard social groups and organizations as having no reality over and above the sum of the individuals comprising them, and to regard social institutions as having no authority other than that conferred upon them by individuals. In tandem these attitudes seem to make social groups, organizations, and institutions inherently unstable. National, cultural, and religious affiliations are modeled on one's voluntary membership in a club, and government is modeled on the private firm or corporation, whose services one may or may not wish to retain. The greater the tendency of individuals to identify themselves with multiple groups and not just with one primary group (i.e. to identify themselves not only with those who share their language and culture, but also with those who share their religion, their social and economic status, some hobby or interest, and so forth), and the more frequently they shift their allegiances (as a result of changes of opinion, religious conversion, changes in economic status, etc.), the more difficult it is in principle to demarcate between groups and identify those that could plausibly count as "communities" in Locke's sense of groups of people who have committed themselves to a certain common political order. The greater the tendency of individuals to see themselves as having no obligations to governmental institutions other than those that they (or at least the majority of their fellow citizens) voluntarily take on board, and the greater the number of individuals who begin to doubt that their retaining the services of government is worth the bother, the less stable and authoritative governmental institutions become, and the less secure are the rights of the weaker members of society who depend entirely on government for the protection of those rights. This latter problem becomes especially acute when the individualist ethos weakens traditional institutions like the family, which comes to seem more and more like just one further "club" one may or may not decide to enter into and remain in (depending on whether extramarital sex, serial monogamy, divorce, etc. are judged to be more attractive options), or redefine according to one's wishes (as with the movements toward "same-sex marriage," "polyamory," and so forth). As the older, stable, nuclear, and extended families which used to be individuals' first recourse in times of trouble give way to ever more fluid and unreliable arrangements, individuals inevitably must rely more and more upon government for their needs, including their Lockean right to at least a minimum of economic assistance when hard times arrive. By the same token, when government itself becomes unstable, they have no one to rely on.

Here Locke's critics might argue that the unintended consequence of his individualism must be a tendency for a Lockean society to descend in practice into one or another kind of Hobbesianism: either a reversion to something analogous to Hobbes's state of nature, where government is anemic and life for at least the weakest members of society is "solitary, poor, nasty, brutish, and short," or (in the attempt to avoid such a result) an opposite tendency for government to approximate Hobbes's Leviathan, as citizens tolerate ever greater increases in governmental power so as to provide for the weak (perhaps justifying such a move by the more expansive possible interpretation of the implications of the fundamental law of nature, alluded to above). Conservatives like the philosopher Roger Scruton would also insist, against Locke's individualism, that the bonds of nationality and culture and the obligations associated with them exist prior to individual choice, and are necessarily presupposed in the identification of any group of individuals as a political community. Those sympathetic to the Scholastic tradition Locke rejected would add to this that the state is a natural institution rather than a product of human convention or consent, and that the needs of the weakest members of society are precisely one reason why the natural law straightforwardly entails its legitimacy. Once again, Locke's rejection of certain elements of Scholasticism and retention of others might arguably threaten his position with incoherence.

Revolution

Let us end our examination of the *Second Treatise* by considering what Locke says about the conditions under which resistance to a government is justifiable. he writes:

> [W]henever the legislators endeavour to take away and destroy the property of the people, or to reduce them to slavery under arbitrary power, they put themselves into a state of war with the people, who are thereupon absolved from any farther obedience, and are left to

the common refuge, which God hath provided for all men, against
force and violence. (T II.222)

It must be remembered that by "property" Locke does not mean
just material possessions, but anything one has a natural right to
by virtue of being a self-owner, such as one's life, health, and liberty. When a government threatens these things, it has contradicted its very reason for being, and thereby lost all claim to the
power which the people had given it, which therefore "devolves to
the people, who have a right to resume their original liberty, and,
by the establishment of a new legislative, (such as they shall think
fit) provide for their own safety and security" (ibid.). The basic
justification for revolution, then – rebellion (armed, if necessary)
against a government and its replacement with a new one – is that
the government in question has violated the trust the community
has put in it. Indeed, strictly speaking it is really the *government* –
supposedly the people's servant – which has in such a case rebelled
against the *people* (T II.226). Who has the right to judge whether
or not a government has done so? Locke says: "To this I reply 'The
people shall be judge' " (T II.240); and "if the prince, or whoever
they be in the administration, decline that way of determination,
the appeal then lies nowhere but to Heaven" (T II.242). When a
dispute arises between the people and their government, there is
no earthly power that can resolve it, and the people may therefore
take it upon themselves violently to resist, with God alone having
the right to judge their actions.

Now as indicated above, given the impossibility of perfection
in human affairs, and given also that there are disagreements over
at least the details of the law of nature, it seems clear that Locke
would not regard just any complaint a people might have against
its government as grounds for armed revolution. Indeed, Locke
says that "revolutions happen not upon every little mismanage-
ment in public affairs. Great mistakes in the ruling part, many
wrong and inconvenient laws, and all the slips of human frailty,
will be born by the people without mutiny or murmur" (T II.225).
It is rather "a long train of abuses, prevarications, and artifices, all
tending the same way" that would reasonably lead the people to

conclude that a government has become basically rotten, and not merely flawed (ibid.). He also emphasizes that it is the opinion of the *majority* that is relevant, not the whims of isolated individual hotheads who take it upon themselves to foment rebellion whenever they feel aggrieved (T II.230).

In any event, Locke's emphasis is clearly on the case where government has failed to do its duty of enforcing individual rights and thereby loses the consent of the community. He is not so clear on cases where either the government is oppressive and yet the majority of the people still support it, or where the people for some reason cease to support it even though it is not oppressive and does its duty. Can the oppressed minority rebel in the first case? Can the people as a whole rebel in the second? Given his emphasis on the consent of the majority, it might seem plausible to suppose that Locke's answer to the first question would be "No" and his answer to the second would be "Yes." On the other hand, the statements from Locke just quoted, about how the people are not likely to start a revolution over relatively trivial matters, were made in answer to the fear that Locke's doctrine dangerously "lays a ferment for frequent rebellion" (T II.224). It would therefore be odd for him to hold that the people could legitimately rebel when a government has committed no injustice at all. Furthermore, since respect for its citizens' natural rights is a condition for a government's moral legitimacy, it is hard to see how the majority's consent to an oppressive government could trump the need of an oppressed minority to have its rights defended.

This naturally leads us to ask what bearing Locke's theory has on the question of secession, viz. the withdrawal from a government of a part of the people ruled by it, who then go on to form a new and separate government for themselves, as occurred when the southern American states withdrew from the Union and founded the Confederacy, an act which led to the American Civil War. It is sometimes suggested that Locke's doctrine of rebellion justified the southern states in seceding, given that they no longer consented to be ruled by the U. S. federal government. The American Revolution itself, which might be characterized as a secession from the British Empire, is typically regarded as a paradigm case of a Lockean revolution. Yet in both instances a Lockean case could be made for the opposite conclusion. For if the "community" in the case of the U. S. Civil War included not just southern whites, but also northerners and southern blacks, it is plausible that the majority of the community did *not* consent to the rebellion of the southern states, in which case this rebellion would be unjustifiable on Lockean grounds. And if the "community" in the case of the American Revolution included not just the colonists but the citizens of Great Britain, then it is plausible to hold that the majority of the community did not consent to that rebellion either. Here again, the ambiguity of the notion of the "community" in Locke's account poses problems, insofar as it allows us to apply his theory of justifiable revolution in a way that leads to contradictory conclusions.

I said in chapter 2 that Locke's project in both epistemology and political philosophy was to defend what could be characterized as the ideal of "ordered liberty," a harmonizing of individual freedom with the demands of reason and morality. Locke's theory of revolution, intended as it was to strike a balance between the imperatives of justice and the need for social and governmental stability, shows just how difficult this is to pull off. And as with the epistemological side of his project, it is far from clear that Locke succeeded. That has not prevented him from having a greater influence on practical politics than perhaps any other modern thinker.

FURTHER READING

D. A. Lloyd Thomas, *Locke on Government* (London: Routledge, 1995) is a useful short introduction to Locke's political thought, and to the *Second Treatise* in particular. A. John Simmons's two volumes *The Lockean Theory of Rights* (Princeton: Princeton University Press, 1992) and *On the Edge of Anarchy: Locke, Consent, and the Limits of Society* (Princeton: Princeton University Press, 1993) comprise a particularly thorough analysis of Locke's political philosophy. Other important studies include Richard Ashcraft's *Revolutionary Politics and Locke's "Two Treatises of Government"* (Princeton: Princeton University Press, 1986) and *Locke's*

Two Treatises of Government (London: Unwin Hyman, 1987); John Dunn, *The Political Thought of John Locke* (Cambridge: Cambridge University Press, 1969); and Ruth W. Grant's *John Locke's Liberalism* (Chicago: University of Chicago Press, 1987). C. B. Macpherson's classic study is *The Political Theory of Possessive Individualism* (Oxford: Oxford University Press, 1962), and Leo Strauss's is *Natural Right and History* (Chicago: University of Chicago Press, 1953). Michael P. Zuckert, *Launching Liberalism: On Lockean Political Philosophy* (Lawrence, KS: University Press of Kansas) is a contemporary defense of Strauss's controversial reading of Locke.

Jeremy Waldron's analysis of the religious basis of Locke's political philosophy is presented in his *God, Locke, and Equality. Christian Foundations in Locke's Political Thought* (Cambridge: Cambridge University Press, 2002). Other studies emphasizing the same theme include Greg Forster, *John Locke's Politics of Moral Consensus* (Cambridge: Cambridge University Press, 2005) and Ross Harrison, *Hobbes, Locke, and Confusion's Masterpiece* (Cambridge: Cambridge University Press, 2003).

Waldron provides a detailed examination of Locke's theory of property in his *The Right to Private Property* (Oxford: Clarendon Press, 1988). Three other important studies of Locke on property are Matthew Kramer, *John Locke and the Origins of Private Property* (Cambridge: Cambridge University Press, 1997), Gopal Sreenivasan, *The Limits of Lockean Rights in Property* (New York: Oxford University Press, 1995), and James Tully, *A Discourse on Property: John Locke and his Adversaries* (Cambridge: Cambridge University Press, 1980).

Robert Nozick's *Anarchy, State and Utopia* (New York: Basic Books, 1974) is the most influential contemporary defense of a quasi-Lockean political philosophy. Against anarchists who suggest that private protection firms could do the job Locke thinks only government can, Nozick argues that even an anarchist society featuring such firms would inevitably evolve into one ruled by a government, and in a way that violates no one's rights. He also defends the inegalitarian implications of Lockean theories of property. I defend these controversial arguments in my book *On Nozick* (Belmont, CA: Wadsworth, 2003). That the assumption that natural resources start out unowned entails a radically libertarian view of property rights is a proposition I defend at greater length in my essay "There Is No Such Thing as an Unjust Initial Acquisition" (in Ellen Frankel Paul, Fred D. Miller, Jr., and Jeffrey Paul, eds., *Natural Rights Liberalism from Locke to Nozick* (Cambridge: Cambridge University Press, 2005)). In "Personal Identity and Self-Ownership" (in Ellen Frankel Paul,

Fred D. Miller, Jr., and Jeffrey Paul, eds., *Personal Identity* (Cambridge: Cambridge University Press, 2005)), I defend at greater length the suggestion that Lockean and other reductive theories of personal identity are incompatible with a robust notion of self-ownership. Roger Scruton discusses nationality and political community in (among other writings) his short book *The Need for Nations* (London: Civitas, 2004).

A Letter Concerning Toleration

Locke's famous *Letter Concerning Toleration* was neither the first nor the last of his works to deal with the subject of religious toleration, but it is the one that best represents his settled position, and which has become the most influential and widely studied. Like the *Two Treatises*, it was prompted as much by practical as by theoretical concerns, for conflict between Protestants and Catholics had been a fact of life in England (as elsewhere) since the Reformation, and the rise to the throne of the Catholic King James II led Locke and his political allies to fear the suppression of Protestantism. Also like the *Two Treatises*, the *Letter* had a profound influence on the American founding fathers, particularly Jefferson, who drew upon Locke's ideas in writing his own *Bill for Establishing Religious Freedom*. As we will see, the doctrines of Locke's *Essay* may well cast their shadow on the *Letter* no less than on the *Two Treatises*.

Locke's defense of religious toleration begins with an argument for the separation between Church and state, which rests in turn on an account of their different functions. "The commonwealth," Locke says, echoing the doctrine of the *Second Treatise*, "seems to me to be a society of men constituted only for the procuring, preserving, and advancing of their own civil interests. Civil interest I call life, liberty, health, and indolency of body; and the possession of outward things, such as money, lands, houses, furniture, and the like" (LT 218). Government's proper concern, that is to say, is exclusively with the worldly affairs of human beings, and "the care of souls is not committed to the civil magistrate, any more than to other men" (LT 218–19). The "consent of the people" cannot give it this role, because "no man can so far abandon the care of his own salvation as blindly to leave it to the choice of any other, whether prince or subject, to prescribe to him what faith or worship he shall embrace" (LT 219). Nor, Locke says, is there any reason to believe that God has given government this function.

The Church, meanwhile, has in Locke's view precisely and only the care of souls as its proper concern, and is of its nature an association that one must freely decide either to enter or to refrain from entering. "A church then I take to be a voluntary society of men, joining themselves together of their own accord, in order to the public worshipping of God, in such a manner as they judge acceptable to him, and effectual to the salvation of their souls" (LT 220). Since the concerns of Church and state are entirely distinct, then, their functions ought to be kept separate. In particular, the state ought not to impose any particular religious creed upon its citizens, and the Church ought not to try to make use of the apparatus of the state, or any other forceful means for that matter, to bring non-believers into its orbit. "Nobody, therefore, in fine, neither single persons, nor churches, nay, nor even commonwealths, have any just title to invade the civil rights and worldly goods of each other, upon pretence of religion" (LT 226).

To bolster his case, Locke argues that it is in any event futile for government to try to impose a particular religious creed upon its citizens. For its power "consists only in outward force: but true and saving religion consists in the inward persuasion of the mind, without which nothing can be acceptable to God" (LT 219). But if genuine and sincere belief cannot be compelled, so that "men cannot be forced to be saved whether they will or no," then "when all is done, they must be left to their own consciences" (LT 232).

Furthermore, if a government could legitimately impose a particular creed, then it would follow that most people will end up being compelled to follow a false religion, for since the various religions contradict one another they cannot all be true. In this case, "one country alone would be in the right, and all the rest of the world put under an obligation of following their princes in the ways that lead to destruction ... men would owe their eternal happiness or misery to the places of their nativity" (LT 220).

In any event, the fact that a group of people holds beliefs that others consider false or offensive doesn't entail in Locke's view that the ones offended have suffered any injustice that might be properly remedied by government action. "If a Roman Catholic believe that to be really the body of Christ, which another man calls bread, he does no injury thereby to his neighbor. If a Jew does not believe the New Testament to be the word of God, he does not thereby alter any thing in men's civil rights" (LT 240–1). This does not mean that every view is as good as any other. "I readily grant that these opinions are false and absurd," Locke says; but "the business of laws is not to provide for the truth of opinions, but for the safety and security of the commonwealth, and of every particular man's goods and person" (LT 241).

Nevertheless, there ought in Locke's view to be some significant limitations on toleration; for instance, "no opinions contrary to human society, or to those moral rules which are necessary to the preservation of civil society, are to be tolerated by the magistrate" (LT 244). No religion could justify human sacrifice, say, or any other grossly immoral practice, on the grounds that it has a right to toleration. And in general, Locke's argument is not intended as a defense of any individual's right to live just any way he wants as long as he doesn't directly harm the life, liberty, or property of another. Indeed, in his *Third Letter for Toleration* Locke says that magistrates ought to suppress "drunkenness, lasciviousness, and all sorts of debauchery" and promote "sobriety, peaceableness, industry, and honesty."

Locke also holds that theological opinions of what he takes to be an inherently subversive nature – such as that kings who are excommunicated by the Church thereby lose their authority, or, more generally, that ecclesiastical officials have a privileged position in determining civil affairs – "have no right to be tolerated by the magistrate" (LT 245). Nor in his view should toleration be extended to "those that will not own and teach the duty of tolerating all men in matters of mere religion" (ibid.). Furthermore, "that church can have no right to be tolerated by the magistrate, which is constituted upon such a bottom, that all those who enter into it, do thereby, *ipso facto*, deliver themselves up to the protection and service of another prince" (ibid.).

These particular limitations on toleration are usually interpreted as having been directed especially at Roman Catholics, since the claims that kings can be deposed by popes, that there is no natural right to religious toleration, and that a Catholic's first loyalty is to the pope (who is, among other things, a head of state and thus a "prince"), were, especially in Locke's day, associated with Roman Catholicism. And indeed, in his earlier work *An Essay on Toleration* he did explicitly assert that Catholics ought not to be tolerated. However, Jeremy Waldron has argued that this view was abandoned by Locke in the *Letter*, and that what he there refuses to extend toleration to are only the specific subversive doctrines mentioned, not Roman Catholicism *per se*. He notes in defense of this view that when Locke does specifically mention Catholicism in the *Letter* – as in the passage quoted above about how Catholics "believe that to be really the body of Christ, which another man calls bread" – he casually lumps it in with other religious views that he clearly thinks ought to be tolerated (e.g. Judaism). Still, both in the passages just quoted and in other ways to be noted, there is a clear animus in the *Letter* against specifically Catholic positions, so that it is surely not *obvious* that Locke intended to liberalize his earlier and more explicit hard line against Catholicism. Moreover, since the specific views Locke condemns were standard among Catholics in his day, his excluding those views from toleration counts as a *de facto* exclusion of Catholics as well.

Finally, and most famously, Locke says that toleration must not be extended to atheists: "Those are not at all to be tolerated who deny the being of God. Promises, covenants, and oaths, which are the bonds of human society, can have no hold upon an atheist. The taking away of God, though but even in thought, dissolves all" (LT 246). It might seem to the modern reader that Locke is simply being inconsistent here. He has already shown a willingness to tolerate other unpopular views, as long as they are not subversive or beholden to gross immorality. Aren't atheists usually as loyal as any other citizens, and don't they typically lead lives as upstanding as those of any other citizen? Furthermore, isn't Locke simply buying into an unfounded stereotype in assuming that atheists are less likely than others to abide by their "promises, covenants, and oaths"?

It must be kept in mind, though, that for Locke the natural law, and in particular the natural rights that are the only barrier between the citizen and government tyranny, rest entirely on theological foundations. If there is no God, then there is in his view no basis whatsoever for a truly *moral* argument – as opposed, say, to a purely pragmatic one – for human rights and thus for the limitations on government Locke is so concerned to emphasize. We will be left with a Hobbesian conception of the state of nature – a "war of all against all" – and thus a Hobbesian account of government as Leviathan. The "contract" that Locke is most likely concerned about here, then, is not the day to day sort of contract or agreement that even an atheist might have reason to respect, but the *social* contract on which civil society rests. While an atheist might happen to respect this and other contracts, he or she can in Locke's view have no *rational grounds* for doing so. Accordingly, Locke's worry is not necessarily that this or that particular atheist might break a promise or contract, but rather that atheism as a philosophy is inherently subversive of the entire moral and social order, and thus cannot be allowed to spread.

Whatever one thinks of Locke's view, then, there is no inconsistency in it. His defense of toleration is always a defense only of those views that are not inherently subversive, and since he has grounds for thinking that certain doctrines – atheism and perhaps Roman Catholicism – are inherently subversive, it is entirely in line with his argument to deny toleration to them. Moreover, his argument is in any case largely a *religious* argument for toleration, not a secular one. Throughout the *Letter*, Locke repeatedly emphasizes that believers' pleasing God and thereby attaining salvation rests on their ability to follow the dictates of their consciences, so that to deny toleration in general is, all things being equal, to threaten believers with the loss of their salvation. There seems to be nothing in such an argument that entails that atheism – which denies that there is a God or any such thing as salvation (in the religious sense) – must be tolerated. If anything, to allow atheism to spread would endanger people's salvation as much as denying them toleration in their religious lives would. In several respects, then, it is understandable why Locke would hold that "the taking away of God, though but even in thought, dissolves all."

Even if it is consistent, however, Locke's position seems to have other problems. For example, his case for the separation between Church and state rests on a certain account of the appropriate functions of these institutions, and his argument will therefore succeed only if that account is independently plausible. But in fact it is a highly controversial and largely undefended account, so that Locke's argument seems merely to beg the question. Catholics, after all, would deny that the Church is merely a voluntary institution whose members can worship God in any way that seems acceptable to them; in their view, the Church is rather a hierarchical institution where doctrine is set by ecclesiastical authorities whose teaching has been handed on to them from the APOSTLES. Locke briefly considers this objection, but in reply offers arguments (such as the claim that this Catholic conception of the church is not biblically based) that would also be regarded by Catholics as question-begging (since Catholics accept neither the Protestant principle of *sola scriptura* nor Protestant methods of interpreting Scripture).

In other ways too, Locke's characterization of the Church is highly tendentious, and decidedly Protestant rather than neutral between Protestant and Catholic conceptions. He emphasizes the importance of personal moral behavior over doctrine and ceremony, insinuating, contrary to the Catholic view, that doctrine and ceremony are inessential to authentic Christianity. He asserts rather dogmatically that there is no one on earth with the authority to decide controversies over doctrine, thereby rejecting, without really arguing against, the Catholic view that the pope is just such an authority. He even goes so far as to insist that "he that pretends to be a successor of the apostles ... ought industriously to exhort all men ... to charity, meekness, and *toleration*" (LT 227, my emphasis), and regards "*toleration* to be the chief characteristical mark of the true church" (LT 215, my emphasis). This simply loads the deck in favor of Locke's view, and it is obvious that no one who doesn't already agree with him has any reason to accept such a characterization of what genuine Christianity requires.

Another problem is that Locke's point that genuine belief cannot be compelled is something of a red herring, for most of those who have opposed religious toleration have not in fact been primarily interested in trying to convert people by force. Rather, their interest was in preventing people from converting *others* to a false religion. The traditional Catholic view, for example, was that it is wrong to force non-Catholics to convert, but that it could be legitimate to prevent them from proselytizing and thereby leading people who already are Catholics into error. For this reason, opponents of toleration would also reject Locke's claim that false beliefs do no harm to anyone; for to convince others to accept false beliefs in matters of religion is to endanger their salvation, which is far worse than harming their lives, health, liberty, or possessions.

Locke's contemporary, Jonas Proast, made the related point that even if it is impossible *directly* to affect someone's beliefs by force, it is still perfectly possible to influence them indirectly. Perhaps I cannot get you sincerely to believe something by threatening you with bodily harm. But if I can prevent you even from reading or hearing about a certain view, then obviously I will make it less likely that you will believe it. By extension, if I can prevent the dissemination of certain ideas in society at large – such as those which might challenge the prevailing religion – then I can prevent people in general from being converted to them. Locke is simply mistaken, then, if he thinks that coercion is useless as a tool for maintaining belief in a certain religious doctrine. (He also appears to contradict himself, since he seems willing enough to acknowledge that coercion can be an effective way of suppressing atheism.)

Proast also objected that, contrary to what Locke insinuates, those who oppose religious toleration do not think that a magistrate should promote any religion he personally *thinks* is true; rather, they think the magistrate should promote the religion that *is in fact* true. As if to anticipate such an objection, Locke says in the *Letter* that "every church is orthodox to itself; to others, erroneous or heretical" (LT 225), implying that since everyone thinks his or her own religion is the true one, there is no point in having the magistrate promote any of them. But this reply seems frivolous, for the same thing can be said about *any* subject matter, not just religion. For example, you might as well say that since Locke thinks he is right about toleration and opponents of toleration think they are right, there is no point in having the magistrate follow either policy. Obviously, Locke would not say this; he would hold that whatever other people might think, he believes he has good reasons to support toleration, and therefore it is reasonable for him to try to see to it that government adopts toleration as a policy. By the same token, religious believers opposed to toleration could say that since they believe they have good reasons to support the truth of their religion, it is reasonable for them to try to get that religion favored by government.

As Proast pointed out, it seems that Locke could avoid this difficulty only by holding that no genuine knowledge is really possible, at least where the specifics of religious doctrine are concerned. And perhaps that is what Locke really thought, even if he doesn't come out and say it. Now as we have seen, he does think that the existence of God, at least, is knowable. But given that he stresses moral behavior over doctrine, that he is so vague in the *Essay* about how exactly we are to know when a genuine revelation has occurred, and that he personally held to a rather minimalist and unorthodox theology, it seems plausible that he did not believe that we really could have any knowledge in those areas where various religious sects disagree. Some of the epistemological themes of the *Essay* may therefore find a parallel in the political doctrine of the *Letter*: where religion is concerned we can know that God exists, but not much more than that; so government should not tolerate atheism, but it should tolerate all sorts of other and more specific disagreements over religious doctrine. Here, again, Locke would be taking a position that is far from neutral, and one that favors Protestantism over Catholicism, the latter of which makes fairly strong claims about what is knowable in matters of religion. But it would at least have the support of the more general philosophical arguments independently developed and defended in the *Essay*.

Still, this does not answer the other objections to Locke's position. As Waldron has pointed out, to answer Proast, Locke had, in his later letters on toleration, to backtrack somewhat on his claim that belief could not be compelled, and to rely more directly on biblical arguments to the effect that we have no reason to think that God intends us in the present day to use coercive methods to bring people to belief. Ultimately, then, Locke's case for toleration is doubly religious: it calls for toleration only for (certain kinds of) religious views, and not for atheism; and it rests on premises that would be acceptable only to someone who shares his broadly Protestant understanding of the nature of the Church and the proper interpretation of the Bible.

Obviously, this opens Locke's view up to further objections, this time from those who claim to support more toleration than he did. In particular, contemporary liberal theorists are inclined to insist that a just society ought to be as neutral as possible between what John Rawls has called the competing "comprehensive doctrines" (i.e. moral, philosophical, and religious points of view) existing within it, with governmental institutions favoring none of them over any of the others. The privileged position Locke seems to afford Protestant theism blatantly violates this constraint.

In fairness to Locke, though, it is not clear that any extant version of liberalism is really more neutral than his was, or that such neutrality is even possible in the first place. For example, even on Rawls's theory, a liberal society is neutral only between what Rawls describes as "*reasonable* comprehensive doctrines," where a "reasonable" doctrine is one which endorses liberal egalitarian political institutions and is willing to ground public policy recommendations exclusively on premises constituting the common ground or "overlapping consensus" that exists between itself and other such doctrines. Moreover, and as Waldron has noted, the conception of persons as free moral agents presupposed by Rawlsian liberalism embodies a substantial and controversial philosophical thesis, not one that is shared by all comprehensive doctrines. Rawls also appears to rule out as "unreasonable" (in his sense) certain moral views that are widely held but which stand in conflict with contemporary liberal sensibilities, such as the belief that abortion amounts to a violation of the right to life and therefore ought to be made illegal. (That, at any rate, appears to be the upshot of certain controversial remarks made in the first edition of Rawls's *Political Liberalism.*) In effect, then, Rawlsian liberalism seems to be "neutral" only between doctrines that are willing to submit themselves to Rawlsian principles, where these principles embody the moral and political opinions typical of egalitarian liberals. That is to say, it is not in any interesting sense really neutral at all, or so many of Rawls's critics would argue.

Now this is not the place to explore Rawls's philosophy in any detail (much less to defend one side or the other in controversies like the abortion debate). The point is only to indicate that it is at least debatable whether Locke's conception of toleration is really significantly less neutral than the conceptions of his liberal successors. If Locke's view entails that religious belief of a theistic and even Protestant sort ought to have a privileged standing in society, it is not clear that this is any less neutral a position than is the Rawlsian belief that only secular liberal egalitarian principles ought to be allowed to guide public policy. We might note also that many liberals today advocate legally prohibiting the public expression of views they regard as "hate speech" directed against homosexuals and religious and ethnic minorities. Whether or not they are right to advocate this, their view is hardly less selective in its commitment to tolerance than Locke's is, insofar as it also refuses to tolerate opinions it regards as subversive of public order. Even if one ultimately rejects Locke's view, then, contemporary readers ought to resist the impulse to dismiss it out of hand simply on the (arguably) unfounded assumption that we moderns have somehow moved beyond the tendency to suppress unpopular views or keep them from having a say in public life.

If Locke's defense of toleration has deeply influenced the way modern people understand the proper relationship between government on the one hand, and the variety of religious, moral, and philosophical views prevailing in contemporary pluralistic societies on the other, it is evident, then, that Locke's view that toleration has its limits is also still very much with us. The difference between Locke and us really seems to be a difference over where specifically to draw the line, not over whether a line needs to be drawn. This is a question that has become even more urgent in the post-9/11 world, where some have argued that we ought to be less tolerant of religious views that seem to foster terrorism. If this sort of suggestion makes many people understandably wary, they will, it seems, find little sympathy for their apprehension in Locke.

FURTHER READING

John Horton and Susan Mendus, eds., *John Locke:* A Letter Concerning Toleration *in Focus* (London: Routledge, 1991) contains several important essays on Locke's theory of toleration. Book-length studies include Alex Tuckness, *Locke and the Legislative Point of View: Toleration, Contested Principles, and the Law* (Princeton: Princeton University Press, 2002) and Richard Vernon, *The Career of Toleration: John Locke, Jonas Proast, and After* (Montreal: McGill-Queen's University Press, 1997). John Marshall's *John Locke: Resistance, Religion, and Responsibility* (Cambridge: Cambridge University Press, 1994) and *John Locke, Toleration, and Early Enlightenment Culture* (Cambridge: Cambridge University Press, 2006) provide detailed historical background to the *Letter* and Locke's other writings on toleration. Kenneth R. Craycraft, Jr., *The American Myth of Religious Freedom* (Dallas: Spence Publishing Company, 1999) examines Locke's influence on American conceptions of religious toleration. Waldron discusses Locke's *Letter* in his book *God, Locke, and Equality*, cited at the end of the previous chapter, and also in his essay "Locke: Toleration and the Rationality of Persecution," available in the Horton and Mendus volume. Rawls's views are developed at length in *Political Liberalism*, expanded edition (New York: Columbia University Press, 2005).

Locke's Contestable Legacy

Probably no contemporary philosopher would rank Locke among the top five greatest philosophers of all time, or even among the top ten. Part of the reason for this has to do with the numerous difficulties philosophers see in his ideas and arguments, many of which we have surveyed. Locke may also be less original than other philosophers; certainly he did not invent either empiricism or the social contract approach to political philosophy, which are probably the two ideas with which he is most associated. Still, Locke did make some significant original and lasting contributions, such as his approach to personal identity. More importantly, more than any other early modern thinker, he combined in a fairly clear and systematic way a number of distinct tendencies which have come to be definitive of modernity: an inclination toward empiricism and nominalism, an emphasis on natural science as the paradigm of rationality, skepticism about authority and tradition, theological minimalism, individual rights, the belief that the consent of its citizens is essential to the legitimacy of a government, and religious toleration. His novel synthesis of these themes is what made Locke what I have called the quintessential modern philosopher, and it accounts for the fact that though he might not be among the very greatest of philosophers, he has, as I suggested in chapter 1, a claim to having been the most influential of them, at least in the modern world.

Within philosophy, this influence was first and foremost on the modern empiricist tradition as a whole, which would not have been the same without him: the work of Berkeley, Hume, Mill, and Russell, to name only the most important figures, may never have existed had Locke not given that tradition the shape and direction he did. In politics, his impact was incalculable, especially in England, in France (where he was greatly admired by Voltaire and other *philosophes*), and in America, where, as we have seen, Jefferson and other founding fathers sought to put his ideas directly into practice. Through the political traditions that have developed in these countries over the last two or three centuries, and especially through the British colonial experience and America's overwhelming global cultural and political influence in the twentieth and twenty-first centuries, Lockean ideas have come to dominate the world.

But any evaluation of Locke's legacy must pay careful attention not only to the dramatic impact made by his system of thought, but also to the considerable tensions existing within it. I have emphasized throughout this book that Locke's central theme was freedom, independence, or autonomy exercised within the bounds of reason and morality – an ideal of "ordered liberty," as I suggested we might call it. As we have seen, his way of developing this theme involves maintaining a delicate balance between several opposed philosophical tendencies. Locke wants to defend freedom of thought and inquiry, and to do so he opposes what he regards as the oppressive overconfidence of Scholastic and rationalist theories of knowledge; but he wants to do so without lapsing into skepticism, subjectivism, or irrationalism. His middle-ground position is that some knowledge in the strict sense is possible, though very little, and that for the most part we have to rest content with justified belief, the paradigm of which he takes to be empirical science. In line with this, he wants to jettison or radically re-define certain traditional metaphysical concepts associated with the schools of thought he opposed – substantial forms, substance, essence, identity, and so forth – but also to retain some of the philosophical theses those concepts were traditionally used to support, especially ones he thought crucial to religion and morality. In particular, he wanted to show, in a way consistent with empiricism, that the mind is in some sense immaterial, that free will and life after death are possible, and that God exists. Beyond these claims, he seemed to think that little in the way of religious knowledge was really possible. For this reason and others, he wanted government to allow for a wide degree of latitude where differences over religious doctrine are concerned, though he drew the line at atheism and other views he considered inherently subversive. In politics more generally, he endorsed the thesis that civil society rests on a kind of contract while denying that the moral law itself has any such basis. In this regard, his view can be seen as a kind of middle ground between Hobbesianism and Scholastic natural law theory: wholly to follow Hobbesian contractarianism would be to embrace Leviathan, but wholly to follow the Scholastics would be to acknowledge that the state is a natural institution, not necessarily dependent for its legitimacy on the consent of the citizenry, which at the very least complicates the case for revolution and limited government.

Overall, Locke's philosophy is that of a theologically minimalist Protestant Christian keen to extricate what he regarded as the key elements of the biblical tradition from the framework of medieval Scholasticism and to re-implant them in the alternative philosophical framework provided by modern empiricism. He wholly endorses the revolutions in thought and practice enshrined in the Reformation, Enlightenment, and modern science, but wants also to preserve the moral and religious heritage of Western civilization, albeit in an "updated" way. Classical natural law theory took the moral and political orders to rest on a natural order that is knowable through reason. Locke wants to maintain the language and some of the content of this theory while abandoning the classical understanding of nature and reason. He wants a natural law without nature, or at least without a "nature" that would have been recognizable to his medieval predecessors.

Locke was certainly a liberal, in several senses of the term. His emphasis on personal and intellectual independence and his eagerness to overthrow various received ideas manifest a free-thinking temperament. His opinions were definitely *avant-garde* in his day, as is evidenced by his need to flee England occasionally for fear of persecution, his decision to publish several of his books anonymously, and the accusations of heterodoxy leveled against him by his critics. He is universally acknowledged to be one of the founding fathers of the liberal tradition in political thought, some of the key themes of which – individual rights, limited government, and religious toleration – are central to his political philosophy.

At the same time, Locke is also a hero to many present-day conservatives, at least in the British and American contexts. This should not be surprising when we consider that what conservatives tend to want to conserve are what they consider the founding or bedrock principles of their particular societies, and for modern British society and American society these principles are largely Lockean. Modern conservatives want to harmonize individual freedom with a respect for the moral and religious foundations of social order. They do not seek to impose the observances of any particular denomination on all citizens, but they do nevertheless tend to favor preserving and fostering a generic theism as a kind of informal civil religion. They favor strong private property rights and reject any suggestion that justice calls for an egalitarian redistribution of wealth. At the same time, they allow for a minimal social safety net to help those who are destitute through no fault of their own. They reject as naïve and utopian the conception of the state of nature associated with Rousseau, and scorn any political doctrine that characterizes the history of civilization as an ever-accelerating fall from some primeval idyll. But they also reject the Hobbesian view of human beings as inherently bestial and in need of a Leviathan state to keep them from destroying each other. In all of this, modern conservatives can claim the liberal Locke as a forerunner.

A tacit Lockeanism may also underlie the attitudes many American conservatives have taken to international affairs in the post-9/11 world, and which have put them at odds even with many European conservatives, whose conservatism derives from very different sources. Locke famously held that "all princes and rulers of independent governments, all through the world, are in a state of nature" (T II.14), meaning that the position of every government with respect to every other one is analogous to the relationship between individuals in circumstances where no government exists. This is so, in Locke's view, "whether they [i.e. 'princes and rulers'] are, or are not, in league with others: for it is not every compact that puts an end to the state of nature between men, but only this one of agreeing together mutually to enter into one community, and make one body politic" (T II.14). An international treaty, on this view, even if it establishes norms of international law or an organization like the United Nations, does not count as an exit from the state of nature as long as it falls short of the establishment of a world government. When you add to these theses the consideration that for Locke, "in the state of nature every one has the executive power of the law of nature" (T II.13), it is easy to see why someone might conclude that any particular government has the right unilaterally to punish another government for its violations of the law of nature (whether these violations involve reneging on its agreements, mistreating its citizens, or whatever). In particular, it is easy to see why many American conservatives would hold that the United States had every right to intervene in Iraq beginning in 2003.

Lockean considerations could even be applied to a defense of the controversial way in which the United States has treated enemy combatants in its wars in Afghanistan and Iraq. For Locke also famously argued that "captives taken in a just war, are by the right of nature subjected to the absolute dominion and arbitrary power of their masters. These men having, as I say, forfeited their lives, and with it their liberties ... cannot in that state be considered as any part of civil society" (T II.85). In Locke's view, since someone who fights in defense of an unjust cause has forfeited his very right to life, he has no grounds to complain if he suffers some lesser punishment instead. At least with respect to those combatants who have engaged in terrorism, then, a defender of American policy could argue on Lockean grounds that there is no moral difficulty in detaining such persons indefinitely or applying to them rough or humiliating methods of interrogation.

None of this is intended as either a defense or a criticism of U. S. foreign policy, which is, of course, not the subject of this book. The point is rather to underline the extent to which American thinking, and the thinking of many contemporary American conservatives in particular, reflects a broadly Lockean worldview. Indeed, a strong case could be made that modern conservatism (again, at least in the British and American contexts) represents a more purely Lockean point of view than that of contemporary liberals and libertarians, who also look to Locke for inspiration. Modern liberals would advocate a far more extensive redistribution of wealth than Locke could have tolerated, in the name of an economic interpretation of human equality that he would have rejected. Libertarians, by contrast, would radically scale back government in ways that Locke did not and would not advocate, eliminating all public assistance for the needy and decriminalizing so-called "victimless crimes," all on the basis of a theory of rights very different from Locke's own. Both liberals and libertarians would eschew the theological foundations of Locke's political philosophy and his advocacy of a privileged place for religion in the public square. There is a sense, then, in which modern Lockean conservatives are really just liberals of an extremely old-fashioned sort – indeed, an eighteenth-century sort – who seek to preserve Locke's moderate liberal legacy "whole and undefiled" against the more radical contemporary liberals and libertarians who would, in their view, distort it by separating Locke's interest in liberty and equality from his commitment to religion and traditional morality.

This does not entail, however, that liberals and libertarians do not have a Lockean leg to stand on, or that conservatives can plausibly claim a monopoly on the Lockean legacy. As we have seen, several of Locke's epistemological and metaphysical doctrines have implications that appear subversive of the more conservative elements of his political philosophy, and of conservatism in general. His empiricism, when followed through consistently, seems to undercut his argument for God's existence; and without God, the foundations of Locke's theory of natural law disintegrate, and the qualifications he would put on self-ownership and on the acquisition and use of private property lose their justification. His rejection of Aristotelian final causes or natural ends makes for an excessively thin account of natural law in any case, one on which the specific content of rights and obligations is hard to establish in any systematic way on the basis of human nature. Natural law theory comes to resemble the caricature painted by many of its detractors, viz. little more than an appeal to arbitrary divine commands. Locke's account of essences and his theory of personal identity seem incompatible with the notion of equal rights for all and only members of the human species; at the very least, these doctrines provide metaphysical support for a moral defense of abortion and euthanasia. His epistemological modesty in matters of theological doctrine seems almost to collapse into theological skepticism, given that he suggests no concrete procedure for determining whether a purported source of revelation is authentic. The rational status of various specific denominational creeds is thereby put in question. In several ways, then, Locke's epistemological and metaphysical views have implications that are far more congenial to the opinions of present-day liberals and libertarians than they are to those of conservatives. It is natural, then, if liberals and libertarians who reject Locke's theism but sympathize with some of his other epistemological and metaphysical views might see themselves as perfectly justified in picking and choosing those aspects of his political philosophy that they like and reinterpreting them along less conservative lines, even if the reinterpretation is sometimes a fairly radical one. Though their Lockeanism is less pure as a result, it may be more philosophically coherent.

Here many conservatives, though they are on the whole closer to Locke's own way of thinking, may for that reason find themselves in greater philosophical difficulty. For contemporary conservative intellectuals seem by and large to endorse the intellectual revolution that Locke and his fellow modern philosophers inaugurated. No less than their liberal counterparts, they tend to see the world in broadly empiricist and nominalist terms, and regard science rather than metaphysics as the paradigm of genuine knowledge. Like Locke, most of them reject the suggestion that belief in substantial forms, final causes, and other Aristotelian and Scholastic metaphysical notions is essential to a proper understanding of morality. They are also, in their own way, as beholden to the rhetoric of individual freedom and skepticism about authority as any modern liberal or libertarian. To the extent that these philosophical attitudes have the unconservative implications mentioned above, then, the conservative Lockean position seems threatened with the same incoherence as Locke's own position. Liberals and libertarians, while less true to the letter of Locke's philosophy, can plausibly claim to be more true to the radical spirit that underlies it.

As we have seen several times throughout the course of this book, many of the difficulties facing Locke's thought, and in particular many of the ways in which his epistemology and metaphysics threaten the more conservative or traditional aspects of his political philosophy, seem to arise precisely where he abandons Scholastic ideas and arguments. It might at first glance seem a promising strategy for the Lockean conservative, then, to consider a return to something like the Scholastic philosophical framework, and specifically to metaphysical concepts and arguments deriving from Aristotle and Aquinas, as a way of providing a more secure foundation for Locke's conception of natural law and natural rights. But in fact, to return to those Scholastic assumptions would be precisely to abandon the grounds for a distinctively Lockean political philosophy. For it would, among other things, be to return to the view that society is organic and the state a natural institution, neither being the product of a human contract. And it would be to return to an extremely robust conception of the possibility of metaphysical and theological knowledge, one which undermines the Lockean case for toleration. In short, in these ways (and many others), it would entail renouncing the broadly liberal and individualistic conception of social order to which many modern conservatives, no less than liberals and libertarians, tend to be deeply committed.

Hence, while there are conservatives who find inspiration in Aristotle, Aquinas, and the broad Scholastic tradition, they tend for that very reason not to be Lockeans or liberals even of a more moderate kind, and they tend also for that reason to be warier than the majority of modern conservatives seem to be of the prevailing moral and political categories of modernity. They may, like almost all conservatives today, be willing to accept certain liberal political institutions – democratic elections, constitutional government, the market economy, and so forth – but they doubt that the liberal philosophical principles on the basis of which most people accept these institutions can or should be reconciled with conservatism. Indeed, from their point of view, the developments in modern society that all conservatives tend to lament   such as the abandonment of traditional sexual morality and disintegration of the traditional family, abortion and euthanasia, multiculturalism and its accompanying social tensions – are all the logical outcome of the basic principles that Locke, no less than other modern and liberal philosophers, helped to embed firmly in the modern consciousness. If the only way to save Lockeanism would be to return to the more traditional approach to natural law, then for the Aristotelian or Thomistic conservative this shows that Lockeanism is finished, for to embrace this approach is just to *reject* Lockeanism.

Leo Strauss might have gone too far in suggesting that Locke was disingenuous in claiming to uphold natural law, but we have seen that there is good reason to think that, whatever Locke's own intentions, his basic philosophical commitments do in fact tend to undermine natural law and the conservative moral and political conclusions that follow from it. Accordingly, Alasdair MacIntyre, rather than Strauss, may provide us with a better way of understanding Locke's ultimate significance. In *After Virtue*, MacIntyre famously argued that modern moral philosophy in general has fallen into incoherence, because it has tried to preserve some elements of the classical or pre-modern moral tradition deriving from Plato, Aristotle, and their medieval successors, while abandoning other elements without which the first ones lose their point. I would suggest that something like MacIntyre's analysis of moral theory applies no less to Locke's metaphysical and political theory, and to the traditions of thought that derive from it. Locke wants to have his natural law cake and eat it too, but this is impossible. Those who seek to appropriate Locke's legacy today must decide which part of it they value most, for they cannot coherently have it all. One must either endorse Locke's revisionist metaphysics – his rejection of objective essences in nature, his mechanism, his reductionist accounts of personal identity and free will, and so forth – and abandon the traditional moral and metaphysical elements of his philosophy, and thus anything that could plausibly be regarded as natural law; or, if one wants to maintain these conservative elements, one must reject the revisionist metaphysics, and also anything distinctively liberal. One must be either a radical or a reactionary. It is no longer possible (if it ever was) to be a Lockean.

Index